Inside the Walls

THE AZRIELI SERIES OF HOLOCAUST SURVIVOR MEMOIRS:
PUBLISHED TITLES

ENGLISH TITLES

Inside the Walls

Eddie Klein

THE AZRIELI FOUNDATION
www.azrielifoundation.org

Cover and book design by Mark Goldstein
Cover photo courtesy of photographer Paul Green www.paulgreenphotovideoart.com
Endpaper maps by Martin Gilbert
Map on page xxvii by François Blanc

LIBRARY AND ARCHIVES CANADA CATALOGUING IN PUBLICATION

Klein, Eddie, 1927–, author
        Inside the walls / Eddie Klein.

(Azrieli series of Holocaust survivor memoirs. Series VIII)
Includes index.
ISBN 978-1-988065-01-4 (paperback)

1. Klein, Eddie, 1927–. 2. Holocaust survivors – Poland – Sieradz – Biography. 3. Holocaust survivors – Canada – Biography. 4. Holocaust, Jewish (1939–1945) – Poland – Sieradz – Personal narratives. 5. Sieradz (Poland) – Biography. I. Azrieli Foundation, issuing body II. Title. III. Series: Azrieli series of Holocaust survivor memoirs. Series VIII

DS134.72 K64 A3 2016   940.53'18092   C2016-903620-0

MIX
From responsible
sources
FSC
www.fsc.org   FSC® C004191

PRINTED IN CANADA

The Azrieli Series of Holocaust Survivor Memoirs

Naomi Azrieli, Publisher

Jody Spiegel, Program Director
Arielle Berger, Managing Editor
Farla Klaiman, Editor
Elizabeth Lasserre, Senior Editor, French-Language Editions
Elin Beaumont, Senior Educational Outreach and Events Coordinator
Catherine Person, Educational Outreach and Events Coordinator,
    Quebec and French Canada
Marc-Olivier Cloutier, Educational Outreach and Events Assistant,
    Quebec and French Canada
Tim MacKay, Digital Platform Manager
Elizabeth Banks, Digital Asset and Curator Archivist
Susan Roitman, Office Manager (Toronto)
Mary Mellas, Executive Assistant and Human Resources (Montreal)

Mark Goldstein, Art Director
François Blanc, Cartographer
Bruno Paradis, Layout, French-Language Editions

Contents

Series Preface: In their own words. . .

In telling these stories, the writers have liberated themselves. For so many years we did not speak about it, even when we became free people living in a free society. Now, when at last we are writing about what happened to us in this dark period of history, knowing that our stories will be read and live on, it is possible for us to feel truly free. These unique historical documents put a face on what was lost, and allow readers to grasp the enormity of what happened to six million Jews – one story at a time.

David J. Azrieli, C.M., C.Q., M.Arch
Holocaust survivor and founder, The Azrieli Foundation

Since the end of World War II, over 30,000 Jewish Holocaust survivors have immigrated to Canada. Who they are, where they came from, what they experienced and how they built new lives for themselves and their families are important parts of our Canadian heritage. The Azrieli Foundation's Holocaust Survivor Memoirs Program was established to preserve and share the memoirs written by those who survived the twentieth-century Nazi genocide of the Jews of Europe and later made their way to Canada. The program is guided by the conviction that each survivor of the Holocaust has a remarkable story to tell, and that such stories play an important role in education about tolerance and diversity.

Millions of individual stories are lost to us forever. By preserving the stories written by survivors and making them widely available to a broad audience, the Azrieli Foundation's Holocaust Survivor Memoirs Program seeks to sustain the memory of all those who perished at the hands of hatred, abetted by indifference and apathy. The personal accounts of those who survived against all odds are as different as the people who wrote them, but all demonstrate the courage, strength, wit and luck that it took to prevail and survive in such terrible adversity. The memoirs are also moving tributes to people – strangers and friends – who risked their lives to help others, and who, through acts of kindness and decency in the darkest of moments, frequently helped the persecuted maintain faith in humanity and courage to endure. These accounts offer inspiration to all, as does the survivors' desire to share their experiences so that new generations can learn from them.

The Holocaust Survivor Memoirs Program collects, archives and publishes these distinctive records and the print editions are available free of charge to educational institutions and Holocaust-education programs across Canada. They are also available for sale to the general public at bookstores. All revenues to the Azrieli Foundation from the sales of the Azrieli Series of Holocaust Survivor Memoirs go toward the publishing and educational work of the memoirs program.

～

The Azrieli Foundation would like to express appreciation to the following people for their invaluable efforts in producing this book: Doris Bergen, Rita Briansky, Sherry Dodson (Maracle Press), Paul Green, Therese Parent, Robert Shapiro, and Margie Wolfe & Emma Rodgers of Second Story Press.

About the Glossary

The following memoir contains a number of terms, concepts and historical references that may be unfamiliar to the reader. For information on major organizations; significant historical events and people; geographical locations; religious and cultural terms; and foreign-language words and expressions that will help give context and background to the events described in the text, please see the glossary beginning on page 57.

Introduction

Walking through the woods near contemporary Lodz, Poland, along the green paths cut off from the city, it is possible to imagine the original landscape of the once small, medieval, agricultural village previously under the control of the bishops of Włocławek. In the nineteenth century, this landscape was transformed into an industrial centre with extensive factories, industrial sites and an ethnically diverse population. During World War II, the Nazi regime reshaped the city of Lodz still more, remodelling it into a German city to be incorporated into the Reich, complete with a new German name: Litzmannstadt. In keeping with Nazi ideology, the Germans sought to expel Lodz's Jews from the city and to colonize it with ethnic Germans from the Soviet Union and the German Reich in their stead. The city's Jews were forced into the Lodz ghetto – the first major ghetto to be established and, after Warsaw, the second largest ghetto of Nazi-occupied Europe. The "Germanization" (and Aryanization) of the urban landscape entailed demolishing the synagogues of Lodz to erase the physical monuments to Jewish life in the city. Jewish homes seized by the Nazis were handed over to German families. Longer-term Nazi urban planning envisioned razing the ghetto and transforming it into a park, a plan expressed in a wartime map but never carried out. The Nazis tried to erase all traces of the Jews of the Lodz ghetto. However, despite their efforts, there were those who survived and testified about their experiences. This memoir brings to life the story of a man, Eddie Klein, whom the Nazis wished not only to kill, but also to erase from memory. Remarkably, he survived to tell his story.

Klein was born and raised in Sieradz, Poland, an old town on the Warta River, rich in history. Kazimierz the Great, the last king of the Piast dynasty, who is remembered by Jews as a protector of their rights, built a castle in Sieradz. Between the thirteenth and fifteenth centuries it hosted numerous meetings of the Polish Sejm, an assembly of Polish nobles enjoying powers that included selecting the king of Poland. By the end of World War I, a vibrant Jewish community had established itself in Sieradz, where Jews worked as artisans, shopkeepers, merchants and in other professions.

Just before World War II, there were approximately 5,000 Jews (approximately 40 per cent of the town's population) living in Sieradz. The German army invaded Poland on September 1, 1939, and by September 3, 1939, they had arrived in Sieradz. The Germans were brutal in their treatment of the Jews there and a number of Jews fled the town. Among them were Eddie Klein and his family, who fled to Lodz, a large city about seventy kilometres away, which they perceived to be a safer place to be during the war.

The Kleins moved to a building on the main street of Lodz, at Piotrkowska 82 (later renamed "Adolf Hitler Strasse" by the Nazis). Piotrkowska Street was aesthetically a gem, an architecturally sophisticated and beautiful street featuring upscale shops and well-appointed apartments far different from the industrialized landscape of much of the city. It was precisely this sort of prime real estate that the Nazis coveted for the German citizens they were moving into the occupied city. Like every other Jewish family on Piotrkowska (and later through the entire city), the Klein family was forced out of their apartment into an unheated room in the ghetto, which was the most effectively closed ghetto of Nazi-occupied Europe. Surrounded by barbed wire, it had only one main entrance, making smuggling or escape nearly impossible.

With the sealing of the Lodz ghetto in May 1940, the Nazis demanded the Jews keep it in order. Mordechai Chaim Rumkowski, a former orphanage director and one of the last remaining members of the pre-war Jewish leadership, who was appointed Judenälteste (Eldest of the Jews) in Lodz by the Nazi administration in October 1939, was assigned responsibility for the ghetto's order, labour and food distribution. With a population of 160,000, this was an enormous responsibility. To coordinate and oversee the everyday functioning of the ghetto, Rumkowski and those he appointed created a large network of departments. Like Rumkowski and his family, those heading the various departments were an elite group with special privileges and access to goods in the ghetto not enjoyed by the majority of its inmates, who were impoverished and starving.

In the summer of 1940, only months after the ghetto was sealed, the Germans sought to "draw out" the wealth of its Jewish population by forcing them to exchange their valuables (furs, jewellery, money) for foodstuffs. This was a shallow well, however, and by August 1940, many had no more valuables to trade for food, and only 52 per cent of ghetto inhabitants had the means to purchase rations. Consequently, large numbers of Jews began dying of starvation. The Jewish leadership scrambled to find other ways to get food to the starving ghetto populace and eventually proposed trading Jewish labour for access to food and other resources. Such an arrangement would benefit the Nazis, who could sell goods produced by Jewish slave labour to German companies, and thereby line their coffers.

Prior to Nazi occupation, Lodz had been a major industrial centre and many Jews in the ghetto were skilled labourers, manufacturing textiles, shoes, leather goods and other items. Therefore the Jewish leadership set up factories inside the ghetto, where Jewish workers began to make goods for consumption by the German economy and the war effort. The Nazis paid very little for this labour and the Jews did not receive money directly; rather it was transferred to the ghetto administration to provide food and resources for everyone in the ghetto. But these paltry payments did not cover much in the way of foodstuffs for the ghetto, as the Germans additionally assessed a sur-charge on items entering the ghetto, which amounted to a "tax" ap-proximately 18 per cent above market rate.

Meanwhile, inside the ghetto Jews were paid not with real money but with scrip, which could be exchanged for food (and which had no value outside the ghetto). Those who were "fortunate" enough to find work were also provided with a meal (usually a watery soup) at their workplace during the day. Klein's father worked in the ghetto leather shop, which produced leather and saddlery for German companies. While working in a ghetto factory was desirable for ghetto inmates in that it provided protection from deportations, it did not provide enough scrip to adequately feed a family. Under Rumkowski's direc-tion, the ghetto leadership experimented with various means of dis-tributing food more equitably, but inevitably – no matter how it was distributed – there was too little food available to prevent mass star-vation. And in the absence of adequate nutrition, disease easily took hold. Hunger and disease were not the only killers of Jews in the Lodz ghetto, though, as deportations to the Chelmno death camp com-menced on January 16, 1942. With brief interruptions, the deporta-tions continued until May 15, 1942.

During that period, nearly 60,000 people were sent to Chelmno. In September 1942, the most well-known mass deportation of Jews from the Lodz ghetto to Chelmno took place. In the *szpera* or "Gehsperre Aktion," from September 5 to September 12, 1942, children under ten, the elderly, and the unemployed were deported. This was a devastat-ing blow for ghetto inhabitants, most of whom were affected directly or indirectly. These brutal deportations took their toll on many fami-lies in the ghetto. Afterward, the remaining Jews of all ages had to be put to work to demonstrate their usefulness to the Nazis, in order to avoid future deportations. Many very young people, including Eddie Klein, found themselves part of the workforce. The problem was compounded by the fact that poor health conditions and ongoing deportations left many teens and pre-teens effectively parentless, either orphaned or without adult supervision. In some cases, children were left to fend for themselves or were placed into a ghetto orphanage under the patronage of Rumkowski. He sought to find guardians for these young people and enlisted ghetto elites who had sufficient food for themselves to "adopt" some of the orphaned children. Such adoptions provided homes and protection for numerous children who were left orphaned by the deportations or who came from families devastated by hunger and disease. They found themselves under the care of those who were privileged enough to be shielded from the worst of the ghetto's deadly conditions.

Eddie Klein was among those who had lost a parent to the great deportation of September 1942. His mother was taken and his father had already succumbed to hunger. This left Eddie, a very young boy, alone in the ghetto. After being orphaned, he was adopted into this privileged inner circle. This was during a period of turmoil in the Lodz ghetto, after Rumkowski had been stripped of much of his power and other ghetto leaders were vying for control. And Klein's position, as the adopted child of Dora Fuchs, a prominent ghetto figure and secretary to Rumkowski, permitted him not only to witness these power struggles, but to develop retrospective insight, particularly into the personal relations between certain members of the Jewish leadership and the elite classes. These elites were in a rare position; they were the "one percent" of the ghetto. By Rumkowski's arrangement, they had access to special food stores that sold goods not available to the rest of the population. And their connection to Rumkowski allowed them to obtain adequate food not only from the special stores but also on the black market, where they could afford to buy food so that their families did not go hungry. These connections also allowed the elite to maintain their positions as they jockeyed for favours through giving gifts of goods and rare foods.

The most elite circles of the ghetto included Rumkowski, along with his wife and adopted son, as well as a web of individuals with strong connections to them, most of them heads of large departments or factories within the ghetto. While Rumkowski's immediate family was known to live simply, others in his inner circle, including his extended family, did not. Mordechai's brother, Józef Rumkowski, and Józef's wife, Helena, were known for living lavishly and she was known for dressing stylishly. Dora Fuchs, who supervised the main offices of the ghetto, was among those at the apex of the Jewish elite. Through her position, Fuchs was able to indulge in foods rarely seen in the ghetto, much less included in the ghetto's standard food distribution system. She reportedly had eggs delivered to her home each morning for breakfast – a pre-war and pre-ghettoization luxury that was unavailable to all other inmates. Bernard Fuchs, Dora's brother, was director of the Department of Labour in the ghetto, and was therefore ultimately the author of the deportation lists. In the ghetto, Bernard had a barber who shaved him and cut his hair and he was also able to support his three-pack-a-day smoking habit, when cigarettes were a rare and expensive commodity. Aaron Jakubowicz was in charge of the Central Labour Office and was the brother of Dora Fuchs' fiancé, Bolek Jakubowicz. David Gertler was the head of the Jewish police and later held other prominent positions. He wielded a great deal of power in the ghetto as an agent of the German police and a rival for power of the ghetto leader Mordechai Chaim Rumkowski. For a time, Eddie Klein had day-to-day contact with these figures, and his memoir gives us rare glimpses into their private lives, the level of privilege available to them, the conversations they had among each other, the dynamics of their jockeying for power between themselves and the Germans and even their private relations with German leaders, relations that were invisible to almost any other ghetto inmate. Eddie Klein was able to see these things not only as a member of the inner circle but as a child he was sometimes treated as though he could not see or understand anything, which led some people to act as though they were completely unobserved. It was very rare for an elite member of the ghetto to leave a candid record of their privileges. While a number of individuals, such as Bernard Fuchs, left oral testimonies of their experience, he downplayed the benefits he enjoyed as a member of the elite. Klein, as a "regular" person in the ghetto, had suffered the loss of his parents and thus had a unique perspective on the benefits of the privileged class. In his memoir, he was willing and able to describe this life, and he opens a window not only on elites' interpersonal relations with each other but also with German officials.

By 1943, the ghetto was engaged heavily in production of goods for the Germans and was largely a labour camp. Ultimately, despite its production levels, a decision was reached to liquidate the Jews of the Lodz ghetto. At the end of June 1944, deportations to the Chelmno death camp resumed. There was a brief halt in the deportations on July 15, 1944. When they resumed in August, the deportation trains were headed primarily to Auschwitz. The last deportations from Lodz took place in September. Klein was among the last to be deported, and he ended up in the Auschwitz-Birkenau death camp.

When Jews arrived in Auschwitz, most were immediately selected to be sent directly to the gas chambers while some were admitted into the camp to work as labourers. There was, however, a third option for some individuals arriving at Auschwitz: a small number were sent to a holding area in the camp where their fate would be decided later. There they waited until they were needed for labour, and thereafter officially entered into the camp, or until they succumbed to the inevitable hunger or disease that took those on the paltry rations provided to the non-working in Auschwitz. This group was also subject to frequent selections. Klein was fortunate enough not only to be selected as a labourer but to be given a coveted job in food preparation. After a short time at this position, he was entered officially into the camp on September 30 or October 1, 1944, and was issued a prisoner number.

Without some sort of special advantage, the survival rate in Auschwitz for a Jewish prisoner was often just a few weeks. Within the camp, such a rare advantage might consist of having a friend or peer who was a more privileged prisoner and could help you get more food or protect you from the worst conditions. Or the advantage might consist of being selected for "privileged" work (not hard labour), where contact with food and other resources might be possible, such as sorting clothing and other goods that came into the camp, skilled labour in indoor or autonomous conditions, preparing food or doing errands or other tasks for a guard or an elite prisoner. Any advantage that gave a prisoner more food and insulated the prisoner from very harsh treatment could help an individual survive longer at Auschwitz.

Klein, already in a unique position as the adopted son of one of the most influential people in the Lodz ghetto, was extremely fortunate again. He very quickly got a privileged position in food preparation in Auschwitz and he had protectors among those he served in this position. His privilege extended to having protectors who relocated him to a subcamp of Auschwitz, which was safer than staying in Birkenau, where prisoners were often rounded up and sent to the gas chambers.

In Auschwitz, Klein witnessed remarkable events that most inmates did not survive to report. He watched Dr. Josef Mengele preside over selections of incoming prisoners, choosing among them for notorious experiments on human subjects in the camp. Klein was fortunate that he was able to simply observe Mengele's selections and was not subject to them, as Mengele held multiple selections of young boys, around Klein's age, at Birkenau in the fall of 1944. Thousands of boys were sent to their deaths.

Klein was also present at Auschwitz during the famed *Sonderkommando* revolt. These "special command units" were the prisoners who were forced to transport the bodies of prisoners from the gas chambers after they had been killed to the crematorium where the bodies were burned. It was horrible work and the *Sonderkommando* were periodically all killed off. In October 1944, the prisoners working in the crematorium knew that they only had a short time to live and plotted to rebel. They contacted the resistance movement at Auschwitz, who arranged to get them gun powder so they could blow up the gas chambers and the crematorium. To gather enough gun powder, women prisoners who worked in an Auschwitz munitions factory placed a small amount of gun powder into their pockets and carried it out at the end of the day. For months, these explosives were collected bit by bit, and then it was passed to the resistance movement, who got it to the *Sonderkommando*. On October 7, 1944, the *Sonderkommando* who worked in Crematorium IV blew it up. Hundreds of prisoners died fighting the Germans during the revolt and another two hundred prisoners were killed after the uprising was suppressed. A number of the leaders of the rebellion were publicly hanged as a warning to other prisoners.

As noted above, Klein's protectors in Auschwitz-Birkenau helped him move, to Sosnowitz (also known as Sosnowiec), a subcamp that produced munitions for the war. They conspired to send along with him a note providing him protection through privileged employment as a runner rather than a labourer. In Sosnowitz, he tended to various German functionaries rather than work on the factory floor. In this role, he was able to get adequate food and remain relatively safe. Nevertheless, as the Soviet army approached in the middle of January 1945, Auschwitz was evacuated along with Sosnowitz. The Nazis evacuated the camps to prevent being captured, with their prisoners, by the enemy. This interest in preventing their prisoners from being captured had a great deal to do with them covering up their crimes. The Germans also dismantled the crematorium and gas chambers at Auschwitz-Birkenau to ensure that the Allies did not find the physical evidence of their crimes. As well, they had prisoners who had witnessed particularly horrific things murdered in order to prevent them from testifying against the Nazi perpetrators.

The evacuation from Sosnowitz was extremely brutal, but Klein's relatively good health and his familiarity with the German functionaries at the subcamp helped him survive the deportation to

Mauthausen, during which over two hundred prisoners were killed.[1] Mauthausen, located in upper Austria near Linz, was built in the second half of 1938. The majority of the prisoners at Mauthausen were non-Jews imprisoned by the Nazi regime for various and political reasons, and included communists, religious conscientious objectors such as Jehovah's Witnesses, Spanish Republican refugees, criminals, and others. Of the almost 200,000 prisoners who were interned at Mauthausen, only 14,000 were Jewish.

In May 1945, the Germans finally surrendered and the Jews who had been held in various concentration camps were liberated. Liberation, however, was not always the end of the suffering for Holocaust survivors. Many, including Klein, were extremely ill by the time they encountered Allied soldiers. The majority of survivors required extensive medical treatment for months and even years after the war ended; there were also a number of people who lived to see the end of the war but did not survive much longer. Survivors, in addition to coping with physical ailments, had to confront psychological hardships from their time in the concentration camps as well as process the loss of friends and family members during the war.

Survivors of the Holocaust were also confronted with the difficulties and challenges of starting a new life. There were survivors who languished in Displaced Persons camps for over a decade as they grappled with where to go and what to do next. There were others who returned to their old towns in hope of finding relatives or to simply go back to the only place they knew as home. Many survivors opted to immigrate to the United States, Canada, Latin America, and other places that had not been decimated by the war. A large num-

---

1   Danuta Czech, *Auschwitz Chronicle 1939–1945: From the Archives of the Auschwitz Memorial and the German Federal Archives* (New York: Henry Holt & Co., 1990), 784.

ber of Jews chose to go to the Land of Israel and help build a new Jewish homeland. Klein was among those who chose to go to Israel. Although he did not remain there, later settling in Montreal, he did work toward the establishment of the State of Israel as a fighter in the Israeli War of Independence and in training new generations in a vocational school.

Eddie Klein's memoir provides a unique window into the lives of privileged prisoners of the Lodz ghetto and various concentration camps. His protectors throughout his ordeal socialized and interacted with the German perpetrators, offering Klein a rare opportunity to "get to know" the "ordinary men" who killed his family, which paradoxically both ensured his survival and caused him great anguish. His memoir bears witness to the atrocities that the Nazis tried to erase from history.

Helene J. Sinnreich
University of Tennessee at Knoxville

SOURCES

Adelson, Alan, and Robert Lapides, eds. *Lodz Ghetto: Inside a Community Under Siege.* New York: Viking, 1989.

Berenbaum, Michael, and Yisrael Gutman, eds. *Anatomy of the Auschwitz Death Camp.* Bloomington: Indiana University Press, 1998.

Des Pres, Terrence. *The Survivor: An Anatomy of Life in the Death Camps.* Oxford: Oxford University Press, 1980.

Dwórk, Deborah, and Robert Jan van Pelt. *Auschwitz 1270 to the Present.* Norton, 1996.

Gigliotti, Simone, and Monica Tempian, eds. *The Young Victims of the Nazi Regime: Migration, the Holocaust and Postwar Displacement.* Bloomsbury, 2016.

Trunk, Isaiah. *Łódź Ghetto: A History.* Bloomington: Indiana University Press, 2006.

Unger, Michal. *Reassessment of the Image of Mordechai Chaim Rumkowski.* Jerusalem: Yad Vashem, 2004.

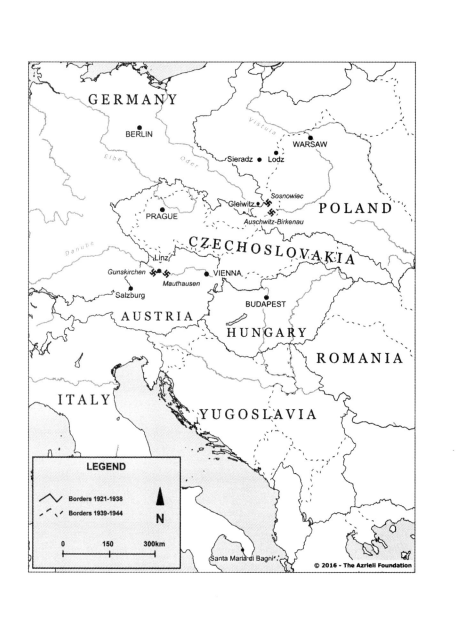

GERMANY

BERLIN

Elbe
Oder
Vistula

Sieradz • Lodz

WARSAW

Gleiwitz • Sosnowiec
Auschwitz-Birkenau

PRAGUE

POLAND

CZECHOSLOVAKIA

Danube

Linz
Gunskirchen
Mauthausen
Salzburg

VIENNA

AUSTRIA

BUDAPEST

HUNGARY

ROMANIA

ITALY

YUGOSLAVIA

LEGEND

Borders 1921-1938
Borders 1939-1944

N

0   150   300km

Santa Maria di Bagni

© 2016 - The Azrieli Foundation

To the memory of my mother, Hela, and my father, Samuel, who perished in the Shoah, and my two brothers, Kalman and Chaim, who died fighting valiantly as partisans.

To my daughter, Vivian, my son-in-law, Itzhak, and my three grandsons, Doron, Gilad and Adam, and to my son, Mark, my daughter-in-law, Jan, and my granddaughter, Hannah.

Author's Preface

I never felt compelled to conclude that I had been mythically saved to bear witness. I did not speak to anyone about what I had been through until the year 2000, when I met my friend Rita at a book club in Montreal. It was then, over fifteen years of conversations, that I began sharing my story with her.

After the war, when, on rare occasions I was asked if I was able to re-engage in normal life with people whose backgrounds were so different from mine, I replied that I knew that what had happened during the war was abnormal. It was a nightmare from which I woke up, and it was the values I had received at home before the war that were determining my course now.

But as time passed, I became aware of reflexes and reactions that stemmed from my wartime experiences. I remember a defining moment in my life when I was in the Lodz ghetto – I decided to cope with what was happening around me by seeing myself wearing a full suit of armour, like a knight in a museum, so that nothing could penetrate and hurt me. Although it was only a moment, it served me, for better or worse, throughout the war, and for worse after the war.

In 1960, when my son, Mark, was born, I realized that I wasn't ready for the strong emotions that reached out from inside me, bypassing my conditioned defenses against deep feelings. When the time came for his circumcision, my parental need to protect him pre-cluded marking him as a Jew, as a potential victim.

I had, at that time, a recurring nightmare: Mark and I arrive at Auschwitz. He is somehow a few years old. I refuse to go into the group slated for work. I want to spare Mark from the sight and hor-ror until the last moment. I carry him in my arms, his head buried in my shoulder. I wake up on a wet pillow.

Flowing Currents

I was born in Sieradz, Poland, a town of 10,000 inhabitants, where about 40 per cent of us were Jews. It is a beautiful area, rich in history, and within the town limits, one river, the Żeglina, flows into another, the Warta. I remember many outings with my nanny, from going to the stream and watching tadpoles, to buying fresh cow's milk from a farmer and drinking some on the spot, to visiting orchards of apple and pear trees and gooseberry bushes.

Generations of my family had lived in Sieradz for a long time. I remember my paternal grandparents, Hannah and Melech, as having a harmonious relationship. As a child, I found my grandparents fascinating. I was intrigued by the story that my grandfather and grandmother were married at such a young age that after the wedding ceremony they played in a sandbox. My grandfather, Melech, wore traditional religious garb, yet was interested and aware of changes in the society around him. He also spoke Polish well, and possibly German and Russian, since our area changed hands periodically.

My grandmother awed me the most. She taught herself to play the piano and did it well. Most of her children – they had seven sons and two daughters – played other instruments and occasionally played music together. She also learned French so that she could read classic literature in its original language. Although she was religious and wore a ritual head covering, this did not stop her from attending con-

2 INSIDE THE WALLS

temporary movies on the arm of one of my uncles. Besides fully participating in their wholesale business, she ran an extensive household. We saw her as brisk and authoritative, but she certainly had to be. I spent much of my time at my grandparents' wholesale business, which was in the neighbourhood in which we had previously lived. It was also opposite the fire station, which fascinated me and the other kids.

My father, Samuel, was the eldest in his family. I remember him as an animated individual whose company was appreciated because of his easy manner and optimism. He worked as a representative for a major Polish manufacturer of soap and cosmetics. My mother, Hela (Helen), radiated a quietness and self-dignity. I remember people saying good things about Mother and Father as a couple, and I have no memories of raised voices or conflicts between them.

My mother was from Konin, less than one hundred kilometres away, and her small family was scattered across various places. In 1938, her stepbrother from Działoszyce settled in Sieradz and married my aunt, my father's sister Malca. I grew up surrounded by the many members of my family who either lived in Sieradz or visited from neighbouring towns – there were almost one hundred of them. I became aware of more relatives after the war, based on letters and photographs from my cousins in Israel.

I know that I was born on May 30, but because I wasn't able to find my birth certificate after the war, I don't know what year. Various documents state 1926, 1927 or 1929. My age was changed out of necessity during the war – it was better to be younger in the ghetto, older in the camps. I do know that my two brothers, Chaim and Kalman, were much older than me, and my first, persistent memory is of them fawning over me. Chaim, the oldest, was the intellectual, with glasses and all; he attended a *hachshara*, a program that prepared youths to go to British Mandate Palestine, in Rovno.[1] Kalman, my younger brother, was legendary for his physical exploits as a scout leader and a daredevil. I was proud of both of my brothers.

We lived at Warszawska Street 15, opposite a convent that occupied half of the ground floor; in the other part lived the widow of a local judge. Our home was close to the bridge over the Żeglina River, as well as to my school. By the time I started school I had already learned to read and write by deciphering business and street signs, and from newspapers. When I began to write little stories and rhymes alongside my school assignments, my brothers encouraged me, as they did with all my interests.

In the first few years of my grade school I was highly influenced and motivated by one of my main teachers, Mrs. Weinterova, a known poet who was teaching in our provincial town only because her husband was a historian researching our area and conducting archaeological excavations there. Mrs. Weinterova convinced my parents not to send me to a cheder, a Hebrew school, in order to keep my Polish unaffected.

I vividly remember my friend Kazimierz and how I met him. I had borrowed a large bicycle and rode it through the marketplace, down a cobblestone street, and then down a gravel road that sloped toward one of the creeks. As the bike accelerated toward some farmers, I didn't know how to stop it, but in the nick of time I decided to ride straight into a haystack, where I became embedded. There was laughter around me, and then I was mercifully pulled out by some of the young men, one of whom was Kazimierz.

Kazimierz lived with his parents. They were so poor that they didn't even own a horse. His father always seemed to be sorting

---

1   For information on *hachshara* and British Mandate Palestine, as well as other historical, religious and cultural terms; significant historical events and people; geographical locations; major organizations; and foreign-language words and expressions contained in the text, please see the glossary.

fruits and vegetables in their cellar. Kazimierz often spoke to me about the farm and its mysteries, which intrigued me. He was quick in his movements and his thoughts. I listened wide-eyed to his stories about distant places. Kazimierz's language was rich and devoid of the roughness of peasant talk. He taught me things about nature and about human nature that I still remember and value. When my brothers were away from Sieradz, I sought out his company even more often.

In later years, I often wondered what had happened to him, knowing that, given the opportunity, his brilliance would surely have emerged in some way. Many years after the war, when I visited Poland, I made some inquiries and was told that he had died during the war. I don't know how. I mourn his death.

∼

In 1939, as summer vacation was coming to an end and I was getting set for my next year in grade school, our city was bombed by the Germans. It was September 3, 1939, two days after the war broke out. My uncle managed a flour mill near the Polish army barracks, an obvious target, and my cousin was injured in the leg by a piece of shrapnel. My brother Chaim had, unfortunately, just come back from Rovno; he had intended to go to Palestine and had come home to be with family before leaving.

There were rumours of an impending daytime gas attack, so we were advised, as were many others, to walk six kilometres to a forest that was located halfway to the next town, Zduńska Wola. For a young boy like me it felt like a game, but by the end of the day we learned that the German army had crossed the border and was moving in our direction. We could not return home, so we continued on foot to Zduńska Wola, another six kilometres away, where we stayed with relatives for a couple of nights.

During the first week of the war, the German bomber planes attacked our area again. My mother and I had just walked out of a building where we had visited two of our Sieradz relatives, the Poznanskis, in their temporary lodgings. When we heard the sound of a siren we ducked through the gate of a nearby house. There was a big explosion. When we heard the all-clear signal we emerged and saw the building we had just visited turned into rubble. The bomb had penetrated down to the basement shelter, killing most of the inhabitants. Our elderly kin, the Poznanskis, perished there.

We continued ahead of the rapidly advancing Germans. At first, some cars were on the road, as well as trucks and horse-drawn wagons that belonged to the Polish army. As the neighbouring towns were bombed, more people joined the stream of refugees. The road was thronged with people for as far as one could see, spilling over into the adjacent fields, such that neither civilian nor military transport could get through. German planes were almost continuously strafing the road with machine-gun fire. People of all ages, and horses, were wounded and killed, and swirls of humanity tried to escape every which way.

For the most part, neither food nor water was available. At one point my father led us off the road and we walked until we found a village; there, my father bought a meal, paying for it with his pocket watch. Then we hastily rejoined the flow of refugees on the road.

During one strafing, my brothers were separated from us and we did not know what had happened to them. Yet, we walked on. We had travelled almost two hundred kilometres by the time we reached Warsaw, which was being intensely bombed. I remember sleeping there on a pile of sharp coal.

This was a new reality we had been abruptly thrust into, where death was possible – and probable – at any moment. I don't remember having the time or the mental energy to reflect on how I felt, but I do remember being scared all the time and feeling lucky whenever an air raid was over and we were still alive.

Eventually, though, I was too tired to be bothered by the shrieking whistle of bombs falling in the vicinity. Yet I had not become inured to witnessing death, as I soon discovered. A loud commotion caught my attention; Polish soldiers were swearing at a man suspected of spying. He was executed on the spot for signalling the German planes. This direct shooting was a different kind of death and, standing just a few yards away, I was horrified.

Near the end of September, the Germans occupied the whole area and the men, including my father, were marched away from Warsaw under the strict guard of a unit of the Wehrmacht, the German army. My mother and I followed the men, as did the other women and children. Many men were shot – we saw their bodies lying in the wet ditches. With growing trepidation, Mother and I walked on opposite sides of the road to check the ditches on either side, looking for my father. Other women and children were doing the same thing, in search of their men. We followed the group toward Lodz.

I don't have an exact recollection of how long it took us to reach Lodz, which was just less than one hundred kilometres away, but I remember at one point coming to a town where we were allowed to join the men. The local Jewish community, very kind and warm people, had somehow secured the Germans' permission to feed us all, and they slaughtered a cow for that purpose. There, for some reason, it felt as though the atmosphere had changed.

Before the war broke out, I had been learning German on my own. After rehearsing the words in my mind, I approached a German soldier I had been observing for some time and earnestly asked him to release my father. I remember "explaining" to him that while for him it may be trivial, for us it was a question of life itself. He responded by ordering my father into the hut from where the meal had been given to us previously. Eventually, when the column moved on, my father was left behind, undisturbed.

The three of us made our way to Lodz, which, with its large German population, was left largely untouched. The people in Lodz were astonished at our first-hand story of escaping to Warsaw and at what had happened there. We soon made our way back to Sieradz, where we found our apartment occupied by German officers. We were not allowed to enter, and I do not remember where we stayed. My brothers, too, came back to Sieradz. They had been apprehended by the Germans, driven into some kind of prison enclosure and had been starved and beaten, but after a short time, they were released. They decided to move on, planning to make their way into Soviet-occupied Poland, and we were to follow.

Poetry and Protection

My parents decided we should return to Lodz. Our relatives in Lodz had moved to Warsaw and their home was available, so we moved into their beautiful apartment on the main street, Piotrkowska 82. There, we developed a friendship with our neighbours Mr. and Mrs. Krykus. Mrs. Krykusova was a well-known fashion designer, very vivacious and charming. Mr. Krykus was a handsome, elegant man, but I do not remember what his line of work was. Within a relatively short time, the Germans arrested Mr. Krykus and took him to a dreaded prison, where he was murdered. Mrs. Krykusova was inconsolable. We helped her in any way we could.

Soon after the occupation of Lodz, the Germans changed its name to Litzmannstadt and Piotrkowska Street became Adolf-Hitler-Strasse. By February 1940, the Nazis established a ghetto in Bałuty, a very poor area of Lodz, and they began to force all Jews to live there, accelerating the relocation process by shootings and beatings. We were assigned to a small room at Gnieźnieńska 29, which was at the end of the newly created ghetto, next to the barbed wire. We knew almost no one there. We had no furnishings other than a couple of iron beds that had been given to us. We had no extra clothes and no money. My father began helping in some kind of business, making a precarious living. He earned enough money to purchase basic items of food, which was already being rationed, but there was enough to fend off hunger. We ate kasha and oil, and heavy, dark bread. A short time later, my father was assigned to a work detail.

Nevertheless, there was a general feeling of optimism that things would soon change for the better. We had neighbourhood cultural evenings, and on those occasions I was invited to recite my own poetry, which was well received by the mixed audience. I remember reciting a poem about a farmer sowing seeds and how the growth of nature eventually engulfed the farmer. Bolek Jakubowicz, the ghetto administrator of the area, attended these events.

As the weather turned colder, there was no coal to use for heat. Most people had already burnt their own furniture for fuel. I rummaged through old garbage heaps with other children, getting satisfaction in finding small, glistening pieces of coal that had been thrown out in better times. I no longer attended school – I hadn't since the onset of the war – but I still managed to read *Jean-Christophe* by Romain Rolland, works by Henryk Sienkiewicz and anything else I could lay my hands on.

My uncle, the flour mill manager, had continued to reside in Sieradz, but he was allowed to travel to the Lodz ghetto, ostensibly to seek medical treatment. He was also able to bring a supply of food for his own needs, and he left a sack of potatoes with us, which was a welcome change from our bland diet. I shared a narrow bed with my uncle, and to make him more comfortable, I spent one night on the edge of the bed, with one bare foot on the cold floor. Afterwards, I contracted some kind of lung inflammation, and I was admitted to a hospital for tuberculosis. My parents were not allowed to visit me but I saw them occasionally as they circled the building, hoping that I would catch sight of them through a window. After waiting for a blood test and an X-ray, I was sent home.

During this first winter, as the walls grew wet and frozen, we had to move to Brzezinska Street, where we were warmer and away from the barbed wire fence and the German guard who occasionally fired his gun. I made friends in our new place. One of them was a composer a few years older than me. He had a girlfriend who was a musician as well. Even though we lived in the same building, we exchanged letters; we promised to be friends forever.

The small apartment where we lived was available for a short time only, and we were next sent to occupy a small room on Zgierska Street, near the bridge. The apartment consisted of a tiny entrance hall and kitchen combination, and another room that was already occupied by a family. This building was close to the barbed wire fence, behind which the tramways for the gentile population moved along freely. However, we were not directly exposed to the fence, as our room faced the courtyard. There was an outhouse in the yard, where people would empty their chamber pots. In the winter the opening to the outhouse would freeze over, and people would continue to empty their pots, creating a hill that grew and froze until spring came. There was no escaping the stench and it was hard to avoid stepping into it. While I dulled my senses to everything else, this sight and the smell repelled and revolted me. I washed every part of my body whenever I could.

Almost immediately upon our arrival to Zgierska Street, we were, to our horror, infested with lice, and there was no escaping the scourge. I succumbed to a feeling of self-loathing, and once, as my father and I stood by the window, I exhaled loudly and told him that I wished that someone would push me into a hole in the ground and bury me. Surprised at my own vehemence, I glimpsed my father's profile and saw a look of sadness and despair.

During the first few months in the ghetto, we received mail from my brothers in Soviet-occupied Poland. They were preparing to come back and lead us to the Soviet Union along a certain route. My brothers specifically stressed that there would be schooling for me there, which was an ongoing family concern. But in the spring of 1940, the ghetto was hermetically closed and there was no longer any mail, news or communication whatsoever with the outside world. The penalty for listening to a radio was death.

Only many years later, after the war, did I learn of my brothers' fate. In the summer of 1940, the year before the hostilities would break out between the Soviet Union and Germany, the Soviets announced that they would register all Polish refugees who wanted to return to German-occupied Poland. My brothers registered, seeing this as an opportunity to reach us in Lodz. After their group had been assembled and isolated, they realized that, under the guise of being a "politically unreliable element," the Soviets were preparing to ship them to Siberia. On Kalman's initiative, they escaped and hid in a forest, joining a group of partisans. When the Germans occupied the area, my brothers acquired arms and fought for their survival and revenge. My brother Kalman was a leading partisan and a genuine hero. Chaim, although very strong and brave, was the intellectual who depended on his eyeglasses, which were lost in a battle. They both died in action as partisans.

I learned of these events from another survivor from my hometown, Felix Kohn. His brother, Nahum Kohn, was one of their fellow partisans and was one of the few survivors of their group. Nahum described what had happened to my brothers in his first letter to Felix, who, like me, had immigrated to Montreal after the war. At that time, Nahum did not know that I had survived; he found out only in February 1956, from one of Felix's letters to him. Nahum wrote that Kalman and Chaim fought valiant, desperate and sometimes brilliant battles against an all-powerful enemy, until, ultimately, they were surrounded. In 1980, Nahum co-wrote a book about their experiences, called *A Voice from the Forest*.

∿

In the fall, on Yom Kippur, we went to a prayer gathering; it was the first time I saw my father dissolve into tears. Whenever we thought things could not get worse, they did.

We were hungrier than ever and we were getting weaker. My father was unable to carry on digging ditches for potato storage, the work to which he had been assigned. I started to work at a saddle factory, sewing leather and making harnesses, and the meagre pay was enough to receive our basic weekly food ration. It was up to us to consume the ration – bread and other staples – when we wished, and we rationed our food scrupulously, but it was a terrible temptation to dig into the weekly supply. The amount of the ration changed every week, depending on what the administration could get as payment for the production of goods for the Germans.

I felt mindless. Starvation was soon rampant, and mortality in the ghetto reached epidemic proportions. Death started with apathy, weakness and the swelling of ankles. The swelling would move upward, and ultimately the heart and lungs would shrink, resulting in a lingering death. On July 2, 1941, that is how my father died.

When my mother realized that my father's situation was critical, she sent a neighbour to come and get me at work, and I came home. My father looked at me for a while, and then he closed his eyes for the last time. He was buried in the cemetery at the edge of the ghetto.

My mother and I were now alone.

~

While working in the factory, I met a Hasidic boy whom I grew very fond of, and I remember him with admiration. His family name was Tochterman, and he was the son of a prominent merchant family who had lost everything. He was perhaps my age but smaller than I was, and he had a compelling sense of justice and a ready courage to fight for it. He cared for others. When I had received the message at work that my father was dying and I rushed home, Tochterman came with me. He was waiting outside when my father died. He provided constant companionship and understanding in the following days and weeks. I'm sure he did not survive the war. I will never forget him.

At the beginning of 1942, the Germans began deporting people from the ghetto. They would make all the inhabitants assemble in the different courtyards to undergo inspection. Men, women and children were separated, and a number of people were then taken away.

At the beginning of September 1942, after an inspection, I could not find my mother. We knew that the people had been taken to Łagiewnicka Street, number 34 or 36. Toward evening, despite a curfew, I made my way to find my mother, to join her. I noticed her with another woman at a second-floor window. We saw each other. I heard my mother express to the other woman her concern about what would happen to me. I was holding the remaining ration of our bread and was able to throw it directly into my mother's hands.

A Jewish policeman, on witnessing this, grabbed me and slapped me around behind a gate across the street. I felt beaten and humiliated. Avoiding police patrols, I dragged myself back to the house. There was no one there. Even the young couple and their child who occupied the other room were gone. At that point, I remembered our friend Mrs. Krykusova, who now had a position in a ghetto factory in Marysin, and whom I hoped had some connections. I went to her in the middle of the night, under cover of darkness, and asked her if there was a way to either release my mother or have me join her. She promised to try. Exhausted, I made my way home.

A few days later, all the Jews rounded up by the Germans were shipped away. My mother was gone. I did not know where to. I stopped caring about anything else and remained in that state for days; I didn't even attempt to obtain my weekly food rations. I had no energy, and I became apathetic. This inaction spelled death.

Mrs. Krykusova came to look in on me and, seeing my situation, took me to her factory, where, as a supposed office boy, I would automatically receive a daily soup and so survive until I got my food rations again. One day soon after, the chief manager of several clothing factories arrived for an inspection, trailed by a group of personnel. He looked at me, puzzled, and said I looked familiar to him. He was Bolek Jakubowicz, who had assigned us our first room in the ghetto and had regularly attended the cultural evenings and talent shows where I had recited my poems. I reminded him of this as he nodded and moved on. My momentary fear that I might be dismissed passed, and I was further relieved when Mrs. Krykusova smiled as she passed me. Much later, Mrs. Krykusova would die in the ghetto, from typhus.

A day or more later, a *droschke*, a horse-drawn buggy, recognizable as belonging to overall ghetto chief Mordechai Chaim Rumkowski, arrived at the factory to bring me to an administration centre on Balucki, or Bałuty, Square. Rumkowski, as well as other important ghetto functionaries, had his offices there. The German administrators of the ghetto occupied other offices on the same square, and it was only here that the Jews had contact with the German overseers.

The whole thing was so sudden and unexpected that I was completely bewildered. Rumkowski and the prominent Dora Fuchs, who was the head of one of the Jewish administrative offices, asked me some questions, which I answered. Other people in the office nodded, and I was taken back to the waiting *droschke* and brought to a lone residential building at Hanseatenstrasse 63, consisting of four apartments, in a guarded enclave. Chaim Rumkowski and his brother Józef occupied the upstairs; Dora Fuchs, head of the main secretariat of the ghetto, and Aaron Jakubowicz, head of the Central Labour Office, occupied the downstairs apartment. Aaron's brother, Bolek, was Dora Fuchs' fiancé. Both Aaron and Bolek had grown up, I believe, in Rumkowski's orphanage in Lodz.

I was bathed, my old clothes were thrown away, and I was given some temporary garb. I was also given a place to sleep in Dora Fuchs' apartment, where space had become available after her brother Bernard had married and moved out. Bernard was in charge of the *Arbeitsamt*, an office that assigned the jobs to the inhabitants of the ghetto.

Another boy, Stanisław Stern, lived upstairs at the Rumkowskis'. He was quiet and thoughtful. We became fast friends, very glad to have each other's company. Teachers were brought in for the two of us. Our lessons were held in Rumkowski's study and taught by a rabbi from Hamburg and another teacher who came from Bernard Fuchs' office. Stanisław and I studied with interest the curriculum devised for us.

In Rumkowski's study, we often had to clear his desk of the gifts he was receiving – poems, drawings, paintings, engravings and more poems, all singing his praises, showing amazement at his genius, and comparing him to the great heroes of history. All this must have fed his already developed narcissism. I think this experience left me with a lifetime suspicion of effusive compliments.

In the late 1980s or 1990s, I paid a quick visit to the Museum of the Diaspora in Tel Aviv. In one exhibit, preserved under glass, I saw many items that looked familiar, yet I knew that I had never been in this place before. Then I realized that these were some of the items from Rumkowski's desk that we had had to move away to clear space for our books.

And so, in Rumkowski's house, I survived. As time passed, I learned about the sequence of events by which I was brought into Rumkowski's house. After the September *Aktion*, the roundup during which my mother was taken away along with many others, Rumkowski insisted that the well-off managers of the ghetto either adopt or provide a home for some of the newly orphaned children. There were two orphanages in the ghetto, and at least one small one with a dozen children who I believe were directly under Rumkowski's care. I gravitated toward them and spent any free time with these boys and girls. Frequently, Stanisław accompanied me. I am still close with some of these old friends – Haim, Beniek, Mira and Walter.

Stanisław reminded Mrs. Rumkowski of her beloved younger brother who had died of tuberculosis in the ghetto. I heard it said that she had married in order to save her brother, but that he was too ill to recover. I remember her quiet demeanour, her intelligence, her tact and her genuine kindness. She spoke the most beautiful Yiddish I have ever heard in my life. Eventually, she and Rumkowski formally adopted Stanisław, since the death of both of his parents had been documented. Both Mrs. Rumkowski and Dora took an interest in the topics we studied and were supportive of our endeavours, often exclaiming "Kinder Freude," expressing their joy at the sight of children playing.

Although I am aware of the conflicting opinions around Rumkowski – who has been researched by historians and has been the subject of many books yet remains shrouded in mystery and much controversy – my own view may be biased because of his caring for orphans both before and during the war. Other orphans, as well, related to me that when they were placed with families, Rumkowski would urge them to tell him directly about any untoward treatment, which he would then set right.

I am convinced that he cared deeply about the Jews in the ghetto. He was devastated when the news was bad, and genuinely ecstatic when something good happened. Anytime he heard the word "ghetto" mentioned by the SS, he would exclaim, "This is a factory, not a ghetto!" He had a certain perspective on our usefulness.

At one point, the SS and Gestapo brought Rumkowski out of the ghetto. We did not know why he had been taken, but when he did not return that night the ghetto population was in despair and panic. It would have been catastrophic if he had not come back. When he appeared a day or two later, there was almost an audible giant sigh of relief.

One day when I was waiting in front of the house, Rumkowski arrived and jumped out of the *droschke* like a young man. He was beaming. He grabbed my hands and twirled me around, then put his arms around my shoulders and said, "After the war, you and I will go to different places in America, where I will give my referaten [lectures]."

At dinner that night, there was talk about the Germans retreating and leaving the Jews in Kovno intact. Now I knew the reason for Rumkowski's exuberance. (However, the liberation of the Kovno ghetto did not actually happen. Was that a deliberate rumour spread by the Germans?) No one else at the table seemed to care much. They appeared to be more concerned with their lifestyle and position in the hierarchy of the ghetto.

Rumkowski's lifestyle was the most modest in the house. By contrast, Aaron and his wife, Regina, pursued a life of excessive luxury and had a second household in Marysin, a small, rural, almost upscale area of fields and gardens within the ghetto. One day when I was alone in the house, Aaron's wife dropped in for a chat. She unwrapped a sandwich and ate one half of it, telling me that it was healthy to stop eating when one was still hungry. (I thought, really?) I had many opportunities to closely observe other important functionaries who let their guard down in my presence, since, in their minds, I was just a boy.

Dora also led a luxurious lifestyle. For example, one morning, shortly after my arrival there, Bolek, Dora's fiancé, appeared at breakfast. While we were eating food I had not seen since before the war he exclaimed, "You see, one can live without eggs!" (Somebody had forgotten to deliver eggs for breakfast.) My father had died of hunger, my mother must have been emaciated when she was taken away, and I would have died of hunger within a few more days. Bolek's statement, despite what I owed him, made me feel like a stranger to these people. Nevertheless, I was happy to be well fed and preferred to eat at Dora's rather than at Rumkowski's, as he practised relative austerity and did not pursue luxury.

Dora entertained fairly frequently at elaborate dinners to which she invited different, but always important, heads of the ghetto administration. I remember how careful Dora was that most of the foodstuffs delivered to her house bypass the records of the special distribution centre for the privileged; perhaps she was aware of the possibility of post-war repercussions. On these occasions I was meticulously dressed and seated at the table not far from Dora. Frequently, I was asked to recite some of my poetry. I wrote poems about the stillness of a cemetery or the noise of a stick hitting a fence. The conversations inevitably led to the workings of the administration. Dora was very good at drawing people out, making them say more than they had intended. Occasionally, someone would look in my direction and signal with their eyes, and the conversation would become less explicit. I understood their caution yet felt bad about the lack of trust. Now that I look back, though, I understand it better.

In that way, I met a procession of people of local importance, the only kind Dora would invite. I do not remember most of their names, just the departments they headed – provisions, police, special police, and clothing and shoe factories. A number of other people there were obviously influential, but it was not clear to me what they represented.

Dora's fiancé, Bolek, who was head of the *Wäsche und Kleider* (laundry and clothing) factories, often attended, as did his brother, Aaron, with his wife, Regina. Sometimes, after dinner, they would form little groups and continue their conversations in hushed tones, which I believed was because of my presence. I felt very uncomfortable.

However, most of the guests were nice to me and even offered me gifts and invitations to visit their factories. For example, David Gertler, a beefy man with an expansive manner, who was head of the *Sonderabteilung*, special unit, on hearing that I was spending much time with my friends in Marysin, gave me a bike, a rarity in the ghetto. I was grateful to him for it.

One evening, David Gertler arrived at Dora's by himself. He spoke boisterously and Dora placed some telephone calls. Then Aaron arrived, as did Hans Biebow, the overall German chief of the ghetto, who came in from his home in the city. At the same time, Dora's brother Bernard happened to drop in for a visit but was turned away at the door. I was told to make myself presentable. David was pacing back and forth excitedly, and when Dora asked him how he had managed all this, he turned the lapel on his jacket, exposing his badge, and answered, "Inspektor Der Gestapo." The truck in which Gertler had arrived – full of supplies – was parked outside. The kitchen help started to unload the stuff and bring it indoors. There were newspapers, liquor, chocolates, oranges and other rare luxuries. David bragged that there was still a wash basin in the truck containing water and live fish. Biebow himself fed me orange slices and chocolates in the merriment of eating and drinking the long forgotten food and delicacies. In the history of the ghetto, I recall this as a one-time only occasion, as a special bonus to Gertler from the Gestapo.

No doubt our voices and the whole commotion could be heard upstairs in Rumkowski's rooms. Both Dora and Aaron declared vehemently that they would not share any of these things with Rumkowski. "Wir werden dem Alten gar nichts geben." ("We won't give the old man anything at all.") I had wondered what role David Gertler played in the overall scheme of things. Now I did not have to guess. This incident also made me aware of Rumkowski's descent from power.

I felt less and less at ease in the house, and I yearned for the honest relationships and the camaraderie of Rumkowski's small orphanage; I wanted to join them. When I brought this up with Dora, she became furious. I didn't understand that my leaving would reflect badly on her. This was not my intention at all. But, I stuck to my decision to leave, and in March of 1944, I joined my group of friends. I still saw Rumkowski often, but not daily.

The Runner

Five months later, when the ghetto was being liquidated, I insisted on being "resettled" together with my friends and on travelling with them to our unknown destination. In August 1944, the ghetto was being hastily evacuated due to the rapid advancement of the Soviet forces. Unfortunately, the Soviet army had stopped at the Vistula River. Dora was against my "capricious" decision and engaged Rumkowski to dissuade me. We talked at length and he accepted my spirited arguments for going with my friends. Stanisław travelled with the Rumkowskis. I heard that they were murdered on arrival at Auschwitz.

My friends and I attached ourselves to a group of experienced leather workers with whom I had worked in the past, hoping to be sent with them to a good labour camp. We took a supply of clothes and were given food, and we boarded the freight trains according to the lists. The wagon was very crowded. There was no place for people and luggage, so we arranged ourselves in a corner on top of our belongings; we had romantic ideas about working and living together and sharing everything.

It was daylight when the train arrived in Birkenau. We were chased off the wagons by the SS. Dogs; beatings; screaming; shots were ringing out. We heard commands, "You go here! You go there!" We were shocked and completely disoriented. The chaos was a terrifying hell.

After an initial segregation we were further selected to go right or left. I noticed a hesitation on the part of the SS man when it came to me, and then he directed me to the group that entered the camp itself. Someone whispered to us that we were going to life, to work. On arrival, we were given a few minutes to undress and hand over anything valuable, under the threat of immediate death for not complying. Once stripped, keeping only our belts and shoes, we passed in a single file in front of another SS officer who was directing his finger to the left or right; at this point, I had no idea what a selection was or what any direction meant. However, I remember a sense of unreality, of being fascinated by that SS figure in uniform. I could not take my eyes off him. I think he noticed. When my turn came, he made a resigned motion that put me in the group of the fitter-looking males.

We were taken to a shower, all our body hair was removed and we were given some kind of clothing. Then, we were herded into a long barracks originally built as a stable for military horses. We were beaten with sticks, threatened at every step, and told there was only one way out of here – through the chimney. Some of my friends were with me in the same block. We were purposely starved and not allowed any rest. We could not sit or avoid the frequent beatings.

In the late afternoon, a large Jewish man, an established prisoner, jumped up on the horizontal oven that ran the length of the barracks. Everyone became quiet and tense; then in a loud voice he asked, "Who knows how to peel potatoes?" People started to yell, trying to get his attention, begging to be taken. But he pointed at me, maybe because I was small and remained standing in the back. As I was passed along to him, people whispered to me, "You will survive. You will survive."

This was one of those occasions where I was lucky beyond reason. The man was a butcher from Pionki who cooked for three privileged camp functionaries. I was taken to the kitchen, which was a partitioned-off front section of their barracks. Across from the kitchen were the quarters of the barracks leader and the *Lagerälteste*, the prisoner in charge of the camp. Between them was the only passage to and from the block. I started peeling and washing potatoes, after which I was given some leftover soup.

Preparations were underway for a party in the barracks leader's quarters. Musicians were brought in, and food and schnapps were being prepared. The *Lagerälteste*, Willie, attended, and at least one of the merry guests was an SS officer. I remained in the kitchen to clean, prepare and so on. Much later in the evening, the SS officer came into the kitchen, very drunk and loud. He requested a glass of water. I handed it to him, speaking German, a language I had used in the ghetto. He was surprised and asked me where I was from and how I knew German. He wondered whether I was a *Mischling*, mixed race, rather than Jewish, and he asked if I spoke English as well. I probably did the stupidest thing in my life when I challenged him bitterly, responding, "What for, so I burn better?" I pointed at the smoking chimneys, visible from the kitchen window. I expected to die the next moment, by being beaten, kicked in the head or hit with a gun as a result of my outburst. Instead, he lowered his voice and said, "Oh, not you, not boys like you. We will teach you a trade, and after the war you will work for the German Reich." Then he was called back by his drunken comrades.

Eventually things quieted down, and I fell asleep in a corner on the kitchen floor. The next morning I was helping to hand out the breakfast ration of a piece of bread and cheese to the inmates as they were filing out of the block. When this was done, I noticed that some of the cheese was still clinging to the very thin wooden slats of the box in which it came. The cook was a decent person and allowed me to take the box and give it to my friends. When people noticed what I was carrying, the box was torn from my hands and in the melee everyone tried to get the cheese. The box was broken into little pieces.

I don't remember if it was the same day or another when, looking for my friends in the milling crowd in front of the barracks, we were surrounded by kapos, guards, and brought to a separate barracks. More and more people were pushed into this barracks until there was no place left, no space to breathe. The doors were slammed shut on us, and we expected the worst – the crematorium – because most of the people in the barracks were older, emaciated or too small for heavy work.

I remember feeling a kind of pain in the area of my heart, a hollow emptiness. At nightfall people tried to sit down, but there was no place. Some tried to sit in each other's laps, but that too was hardly possible, and people were fighting for a little space for themselves. Suddenly, the door was opened; we heard yelling in German, and the beam of a flashlight being shone into one row after another startled us. The light blinded me as I was pulled out from where I was standing and pushed toward the entrance. There I heard that same SS officer who had come into the kitchen, drunk. He and the chief kapo, a lame German prisoner by the name of Karl, brought me to another barracks. I never saw this officer again.

The next day, the *Lagerälteste*, Willie, took me through the length of the camp. We came close to the train tracks, where there was a barracks for sorting clothes and doing some tailoring. On the way, he stopped at one of the barracks and demanded to see an inmate, a Dutch Jew, who was a recent arrival. Willie started to beat this man with a walking cane. As the man cried out with pain, Willie kept asking him if he had screamed when he was betraying his fellow Jews in Theresienstadt. The beating continued for some time. Later we went to the clothing workshop, and on the way back he stopped at the same barracks again and continued to beat the man.

I later heard that Willie had, as a criminal, been imprisoned for many years. Supposedly, he had been a ship's captain and had sold a part of his cargo for the sake of some romantic affair. I also heard that Willie had been a frequent visitor to the *Familienlager*, where Czech Jews from the Theresienstadt transports had been kept. In March or July 1944, when the Jews in this camp were undergoing selection and thousands were sent to be gassed, he and Karl had apparently managed to pull out about a hundred young boys and transfer them to the men's camp.

I was given a place to sleep in the *Schreibstube*, an administrative office that was the block closest to the SS guards. It was occupied by the camp scribes, and was near the barracks of the prisoners called the Kanada *Kommando*, whose job was to unload what remained on the trains after the people were taken away.

At some point, I was relieved to receive a prisoner number – B11104 – tattooed on my arm. Daily, I had been witnessing large numbers of people being taken to the gas chambers directly from the incoming trains, which we could see from the camp. Having my name registered and a number on my arm, although guaranteeing neither privileges nor survival, gave me a feeling of having a distinct identity rather than that of being a particle of a nameless mass. That is how I felt at that time. Willie told me that he had ordered that my number be the smallest possible size ever given in Auschwitz. I also received properly fitting clothing.

Being tattooed and numbered, I was now given permission to enter the other camps in Birkenau. My job was to be ready at any time to carry messages from the SS at the entrance of the former *Zigeunerlager* camp – where thousands of Roma prisoners had been held – to different barracks or to kapos, work details or workshops. I was also given the task of feeding the rabbits that were being raised by an SS man. I had to collect little plants growing along the barbed wire. Under the guise of collecting more of the sparsely growing greens, I could learn more about the place.

Close to us was the *Krankenbau*, an infirmary, which was not really a building for the sick but was actually a holding tank for the gas chambers. Some people, however, were returned from the *Krankenbau* to the camps. Further away were the crematoria. Beside us was another rectangular camp like ours, called the *Arbeitslager*, the work camp. One of the enclosures was the women's quarantine camp. My aim was to enter the camps where the women who had arrived from the Lodz ghetto were kept. I was trying to locate an artist, Mrs. Feldman, who was, for a time, working at the small orphanage in the ghetto and whom I admired greatly. I met several women I knew from the ghetto, but I did not succeed in finding Mrs. Feldman.

This was a time of reprieve for me. I was known, and not threatened by the different SS and kapo. On the contrary, I could even help others and, in the face of all of our looming deaths, I considered this a personal mission. Once, when Dr. Mengele ordered me to carry a message and to return with a reply, I, of course, obeyed the order, at desperate speed. He called me *Schwung*, swift, and others began calling me by that name, too.

Periodically, Dr. Mengele came to the camp with a pretty young woman who carried artist's supplies. While he was busy selecting people for life or death, she waited where I was stationed. I assume that at other times she was required to draw facial characteristics of twins, who were kept for the purpose of his research. While she and I were waiting together, we had long conversations; our talks left me with the impression that what she did so often left her with no illusions about our chances of survival. This reinforced my conviction of imminent death, despite my temporary reprieve. I thought I would never know her eventual fate, though I did find out much later, by chance, that she did survive.

In the late 1970s, I was in Sarasota, Florida, sitting with friends near a swimming pool when we were joined by a couple, Eva and Ruda Roden. Eva turned to me and, noting my tattooed number, remarked that she too had been in Birkenau, in the *Familienlager*. I told Eva about the artist who was from the *Familienlager,* and how I carried her in my psyche because of her sadness. I said that I didn't remember her name, and was sure that I would never know her fate. Eva turned to her husband and said, "He is talking about Dina Gottliebova."

They then told me that she was living in Anaheim, California, and was working for Walt Disney. In my subsequent correspondence and telephone conversations with Dina, she related to me her desire to recover at least three of the paintings of Gypsies (Roma) that she had done on the orders of Mengele, paintings that are currently located at the Auschwitz-Birkenau State Museum. As far as I know, she did not recover them before she passed away.

Landscape of Death

One day, around the beginning of October, we heard a commotion. There had been a rebellion by one of the crematorium groups, the *Sonderkommando*. They were apprehended and brought to our camp, surrounded by SS officers and dogs. The next morning they were marched again to the very installations where they had worked. They communicated to us with their eyes and circling fingers that they were being taken to go up in smoke. I think they were the group who had succeeded in blowing up one of the crematoria.

Rumours started about upcoming changes in the camp, and at one time a convoy of cars brought a special SS unit from outside of Auschwitz. There was fear and trepidation even among the established prisoners in the camp. A Ukrainian prisoner who had apparently been released was among them as an "honorary prisoner." I heard that he had something to do with a political assassination in the Ukraine before the war.

Afterwards, Willie, the camp leader, told me that he had decided to transfer me to Buna, a nearby factory camp that produced ammunition. Later, Willie and Karl told me that this was not such a good idea after all, and they decided instead to send me to a camp in Sosnowiec. Willie procured a letter from an SS officer for me to hand over to the SS Commandant in Sosnowiec. Sometime around the end of 1944, I arrived there with a small group and was received in an orderly fashion. I presented the letter I was given to the Commandant, who was a portly, grandfatherly figure and who immediately proclaimed that if I was good enough to be a runner in Birkenau, I was good enough to be a runner for him in Sosnowiec. At a later date, I heard that he had attained his rank as Commandant in the infamous camp of Dachau. This was an unsettling thought.

Sosnowiec was a work camp, and it was well organized and clean. There were no beatings or outright starvation in this camp. The main kapo was a Jew from Germany, an intellectual type, quite decent and fair. His younger brother became my friend. The inmates were marched to a factory that manufactured barrels for cannons and machine guns. The contrast between Auschwitz and Sosnowiec is hard to describe. Still, there was no guarantee of what tomorrow would bring.

I learned the gist of my duties quickly, since the camp was not large. Besides being a runner carrying messages, I had to stoke the fires from dawn to night in the offices and in the individual quarters of the SS Commandant and the SS *Rapportführer*, as well as the other SS men. All of them had private quarters. I had enough food and sometimes was given meals from the SS kitchen.

Whenever there was time, I tinkered in the camp's maintenance machine shop, and I built a reading lamp for the SS Commandant. When I was taking it to him, a young SS man stopped me and asked me what I was carrying. As he admired the lamp, I immediately offered it to him. When he said I shouldn't give it to him since it was for the Commandant, I offered to make one for him as well, which I did.

I was privy to conversations among the SS, and sometimes between the *Rapportführer* and the *Lagerälteste*. I learned that Germany was being bombed to smithereens and that the Allied forces were advancing steadily.

At Christmas, the SS Commandant's family came over. A Christmas tree was put up, and gifts were placed under the tree that I had decorated. To my surprise, there were gifts from the family to me, and they had wrapped the lamp I had made for the Commandant, presenting it to him as a gift from me. So soon after Birkenau, I was forgetting what a concentration camp could be. I was lulled by the uneventful flow of days in the work camp.

During Christmas, as I was stoking the fire in a room of one of the older SS officers, he started to cry pitifully that he had not received a letter from his wife and daughter in Austria; he said that he was worried they may have come to some harm from a bombing. He told me that his unit had distinguished itself on the Eastern front and as a reward had been attached to the SS, and that was how he had come to be a guard in Sosnowiec. When he accompanied the inmates going to work, he would ask them politely to keep a straight line. I remember putting an arm on his shoulders, telling him not to cry, that it was probably just that the post office could not manage the workload.

On that same Christmas holiday, when I came to stoke the fire in a younger SS man's room, he was in bed, appearing to be asleep, and lying beside him was a naked woman. She was the leader of a girls' Hitler group. My presence didn't seem to wake them, or they simply chose to ignore me. Later, when I brought coal to the *Rapportführer*'s room, he and his mistress were sitting up in bed, and she was not very well covered. They watched me with amusement and smiles, called me over and showed me French erotic postcards, one by one, watching my expression. The *Rapportführer* then said he must take me at the next opportunity to a public house. When I related this story to a man in a bunk next to mine, he told me that they had actually taken him to a place like that. This man was a young French navy officer. He was wounded and lame but was treated with respect while doing bookkeeping for the SS.

I practically had the run of the place and, on occasion, when the telephone rang in the Commandant's office, I simply answered it and related the message either verbally or in writing. I asked permission from the Commandant to visit the factory, which I did more than once. I would be escorted with others and would return the same way. There were some interesting machines there, and to this day I know the ins and outs of making spiral grooves in a gun barrel.

What really fascinated me, though, was that for the first time in five years I saw a group of young Polish civilian men and women who were working in the factory. One beautiful Polish girl with a harmonious voice was working at a desk in the middle of the factory floor. Whenever possible, she read a book of poems, and although she was a few years older than I, we found a lot in common. Her approval of me made me very acceptable to the whole group of the Polish civilian workers.

She must have noticed the effect she had on me. I was not hungry or tired, nor immediately threatened at that time, and I couldn't get her out of my mind. I think she was toying with me, but she also took some gentle initiatives, in touching my hand and arm and looking at me with very knowing eyes. She told me that the young men I saw disappearing, ostensibly to the protectorate that was a part of Poland not annexed to the Third Reich, were actually going to join partisans.

When she agreed to arrange for my escape to the partisans, I appealed to the Commandant that I wanted to learn a trade in order to be useful in the future and to work in the factory rather than be a runner in the camp. I assured him that I would still fulfill most of my duties after work. He gave me permission to do so. My first work shift started at night. The plan for my escape now became more realistic. One difficulty was that in a single night we would have to cover more than thirty kilometres of forest trails to reach the communist partisans. It was intimated to me that the other groups closer to Sosnowiec were not safe for me because I was a Jew.

The reports of the Soviets progressing were very encouraging, and at one time a group of Polish workers sat in a corner, humming "The International," and a German foreman in the factory sang, "Es geht alles vorüber, es geht alles vorbei, geht auch der Hitler mit seiner Partei." (Everything ends, everything passes, and so will Hitler [along] with his Party.)

At one point, we could hear guns in the distance. The Soviets were getting closer. I felt great apprehension in the face of my choices: Should I risk my escape? Should I put my complete trust in the Poles who were sympathetic to me? I knew we would have to pass close to the hostile partisan units.

Soon it was all moot. In mid-January, one morning at dawn, we were assembled in a hurry. We did not go to the factory. The SS loaded their belongings in wagons, and we set out away from the front. We began a long, wintry trek on foot. We walked in columns on snow-covered ground, with little food and at a fast pace. Whoever could not keep up was shot. We went toward Gleiwitz, where the elderly SS camp Commandant had his home and family, whom I had met at Christmas. The Soviet front was advancing behind us. We could still hear the artillery barrage. A thought occurred to me, to ask the Commandant to let me hide in the wagon with his belongings and remain hidden with his family until the area changed hands. Had I done it, and survived, I would have saved myself the horror I was yet to experience. The worst was yet to come.

Our march continued without the Commandant. Once, we slept in a slaughterhouse and meat processing plant. We found some fat there to scrape off and eat. The young SS man to whom I had given the lamp in Sosnowiec proved to be an enthusiastic murderer, shooting all who were weakened and could not keep up during the march. This very same man also occasionally shared his bread with me. Once, he brought me his long military coat in order to wash out some blood-spattered stains. As I was washing them out mechanically, the monstrosity of it turned my insides. I was dead tired.

That night, everyone was already asleep in a barn that had been made available to us. I returned the cleaned coat to some kind of a large room where the SS officers were sprawled out on the floor, sleeping. A wild idea struck me: Near a sleeping SS man, only two steps away from me, lay a grenade; if I could throw it, maybe I could change my fate and that of the others, and we could wait for the Soviet front to overtake us. The grenade was a cylindrical object with a long handle called a Panzerfaust. I really did not know how to activate it, and the heady moment passed.

The next day, more SS men appeared and surrounded us. The young SS man and the Austrian who had once cried with fear for his family continued with us. After approximately two weeks of marching and sleeping mostly on snowy ground, we reached a train station. We were loaded into cattle wagons and were shuttled around. After four days, whoever could still stand was marched into Mauthausen. It was only later that I learned that Mauthausen was classified as a Category III camp, designated for prisoners charged with serious crimes; in actuality it meant that the camp was notorious for its brutality and harsh punishments.

It was the beginning of February 1945, and the real fight for survival from day to day, hour to hour, started then. Had I known what was to come, I would not have hesitated on those doubtful occasions I had to escape. I remember walking uphill into the camp enclosure. Then, a selection occurred, a chaotic movement of people back and forth in a narrow space, with beating and yelling. The men who survived this ordeal were brought into a barracks; whoever couldn't go on was left behind. They were either finished or being finished off. The barracks at Mauthausen were more orderly than at Birkenau. We were counted inside the barracks and were assigned numbers. Mine was 125482.

On a second roll call I fainted, but I was momentarily held up by two adult prisoners, one on either side of me. Later on, a doctor, who was a prisoner, came by and looked at the four very large boils under my left arm, which had developed during our trek before we got on the train, maybe from sleeping most of the time outside on the frozen ground.

Together with a group of about fifteen other prisoners I was taken to the so-called hospital camp, called *Russenlager*, the Russian Camp. This was one of the ways of being put to death in Mauthausen. Prisoners with any kind of illness were brought to the *Russenlager*, placed five and six to a bunk, and left to die. Often their death was hastened by beatings, by gasoline injections, or by dunking their heads into a barrel of chlorinated water at the back of the block where the wagons were collecting their steady flow of dead bodies. *Russenlager*, I knew, was a dreaded destination, but it was only later that I learned most of the details.

On the way to the *Russenlager*, my group passed by an open square where the previously mentioned *Lagerälteste* from Sosnowiec was conversing with a local Austrian kapo. On seeing me, he asked his kapo friend where the group was going. After exchanging some words, they conferred with the Yugoslavian prisoner who was leading us. We moved on. On arrival I was separated from the others. Eventually, a German corporal or sergeant approached me and told me to lie down on a stone slab of a table. He applied something on my boils and started to cut. I kept losing consciousness from the pain. I noticed some kind of spray. I don't know when I was led back to the block.

I assumed this intervention on my behalf had taken place because of a request from the German *Lagerälteste* from Sosnowiec to his friend the Austrian kapo. Incidentally, after the war, I found out that the authorities at Mauthausen had presumed my death in the *Russenlager* – through the Jewish Genealogical Society, I obtained a copy of my death certificate from Yad Vashem, which had actually been issued at Mauthausen.

I was given a chance to recuperate by receiving permission to lie on the floor instead of standing outside in the freezing February weather. My food was given to me on the floor, and on some roll calls I was counted without having to stand up. I became friendly with some Polish prisoners in the block, who brought me additional food and marvelled at my survival. I reciprocated by reciting some Polish poetry. I never saw the Sosnowiec German again but was visited twice by the Austrian kapo who was in charge of some tailoring enterprise, where imprisoned Jehovah's Witnesses were working. I was growing stronger.

At some point, I somehow incurred the wrath of the *Blockälteste*, an Austrian criminal who watched for me as we were filing out of the block for a general roll call, the counting of the prisoners. He tried to smash my head with a heavy stool. I managed to jump out of the way, avoiding his blow, and run to the roll call square. During the hours of roll call, I was trying to mentally prepare for the end of my life upon my return to the block. I heard that two days earlier he had killed a Hungarian boy in the washroom.

That afternoon, the Jews were segregated and sent to a separate so-called lower camp in Mauthausen. We never returned to the previous camp. Fortunately, the new camp was out of reach of the murderous *Blockälteste*, and so I escaped being killed. We remained there for days, freezing outside, huddling together for warmth, with the stronger people pushing constantly for a place in the centre, where it was warmer. I stood near a cold wall. We were then transferred to yet another fenced-off area, outside the main camp, and were pushed into a number of large circus tents.

In the tent camp, organization broke down. Most of the time, the garbage cans containing some soup slop were placed near the entrance. Anyone who could fight for it did. I remember eating some bread. There wasn't enough space inside the tents for all of us, and thousands more people kept arriving. Incredibly, the newcomers included women and some children. They were all dressed in civilian clothes. Some of them still had watches and other valuables, while others were destitute. These people were mostly Hungarian Jews who had dug trenches for the Germans on the front line. The trek to the camp and the ongoing starvation hit them very hard. Most arrived weakened, disoriented and at the end of their wits. Many were dying, and others who could still move were forced to stack up the corpses like cordwood in large rectangular heaps, since the burning pits could not keep up. We were inured to the sight of dying men, but it was a shock to watch husbands, wives and children dying in sight of each other, their bodies turning the expanse of the camp into a landscape of death.

One day in the spring, we were marched to a forest near Wels; along the road, many people fell by the wayside. The weather turned warmer, and the nights were extraordinarily beautiful. Spring was here and I allowed myself to dream about being a gypsy and travelling the back roads and fields. We ate snails that we found on the blades of grass and even had some red salt that one of the prisoners had in his pocket. He mentioned it was from the crematorium. In April 1945, we, the surviving marchers, arrived in Gunskirchen.

I don't know how many of us made it to that point. The place was already crowded beyond belief, worse than anything I had experienced before. It began raining, endlessly. Those who could tied themselves to the overhead rafters with their belts and did not leave their perches for any reason. It was hard to make one's way out, but to come back into the shelter was almost impossible. I remember getting some food whenever I could make it to the distribution point – ten decagrams of bread overgrown with mould and a small quantity of some watery soup. With no time frame, I don't know how many weeks we were there.

Then the SS left their posts.

The Americans came at the beginning of May, at which time I was lying on the outside heap of people at different stages of dying. All remaining strength had left me. I remember two youngsters whom I had seen before – from the transport from Mauthausen to Gunskirchen – sharing a can of Red Cross condensed milk that they had discovered in the German kitchen, as well as bits of other food, items for which they had probably had to fight. They looked at each other, then at me, and agreed to share with me the life-giving food. I was too tired to speak and thanked them with my eyes.

In Wels, I contracted typhus. Gravely ill, I was taken to a hospital in the American-occupied city of Linz. There were over thirty of us on the ground level hall, and many continued to die all around me.

At the end of May, I was still not out of the woods. Somewhere in my delirium I must have mentioned that my birthday was on May 30, and on that day a nurse brought me a beautiful birthday card. I was amazed at that human touch, and for the first time since the beginning of the war, I cried and cried for a very long time.

A Touch of Levity

For a time, I felt numb. At no point did I feel joyful or exuberant. I guess one needs physical and mental energy to have these emotions. I didn't notice anyone else in a celebratory mood either. I remember living in military barracks in Austria, in either Wels or Linz, named the Alpenjager Caserne. Upon my recovery I sought and received a paper from a US official at the city hall, which allowed me to travel in search of my mother.

A stream of people – released prisoners, civilians of different countries, as well as military prisoners – was moving in all directions. First I had to find a reliable source of information to give me a clue as to where to start looking. I came across a Swiss legation making a list of youngsters who wanted to go to Switzerland, and they registered my name. The group for Switzerland was being assembled, and I stayed with them for a couple of days. In another town a group was being formed to go to the United States. I was advised to put my name down with them as well and to lower my age in order to fit into a school program. The third choice was England. Staying with any one of these groups was acknowledging that my mother was not alive, so I moved on to continue my search.

I came across a soldier surrounded by an excited group of people, all speaking Yiddish. This was a member of the Jewish Brigade, which was under the command of the British Eighth Army. Other Jewish soldiers from Palestine arrived to organize a group to be taken to British Mandate Palestine as soon as the means became available. Seeing these soldiers brought back memories of my family's involvement with Zionism and the many endearing stories and anecdotes about Eretz Yisrael I had listened to at the family dinner table. I learned from the soldiers about the existence of a bureau in Jerusalem dedicated to finding and uniting relatives, survivors of the Hitler period. The name of the bureau, and its radio program, was *Ha'Mador Le'hipus Krovim*, Searching for Dear Ones. They told me that the Jews of Eretz Yisrael were waiting with open arms and a place in their hearts for us, the remnants. My memories of the Zionist organizations and the ardent idealism, Zionist and socialist at once, gave me the feeling of being given a directive that I needed to follow without hesitation.

On July 10, 1945, the soldiers smuggled our group over a border near Salzburg in military trucks with lowered tarpaulins and brought the whole group to the town of Santa Maria di Bagni in southern Italy. We arrived at night and slept in an empty villa that had been taken from a fascist. The villa was on top of a hill, and down the road I could see the sea glistening in the morning sun; the array of different colours was incredibly alluring. As I approached the shore I saw two Italian men conversing; then, one of them paused, dove leisurely, sideways somehow, into the bay, and came up with something to eat, which he shared with his friend, continuing to converse.

We were called for breakfast, and I walked down the street to a field kitchen and was given regular, basic food. This was repeated at lunch and dinner. The vineyards at the side of the road were laden with dark grapes, and in the back of the villa was a large fig tree with ripening fruit. In the evening we sat on the wide steps of the villa. The sky was heavy with stars, and unfamiliar aromas wafted in on the light breeze. While the Italian families were placing their chairs on one side of the street on the almost nonexistent sidewalks, someone down the street started to sing "Mamma." "Mamma, son tante felice…." It seemed that the whole village took it up – different voices, singing beautifully, like a choir. I have never spoken to my friends of this magical evening, but I think we all felt then that maybe healing was possible.

~

I was reunited with my friends Haim and Beniek from the ghetto, who were in a separate group in another building. Haim, with his perfect knowledge of Hebrew, was actually in charge of Beniek's group. There was also a group of girls.

Dr. Skulnick, an officer in the Jewish Brigade, was in charge of cultural events. An educator from Tel Aviv, he organized daily activities. The main focus was writing articles and contributing them to our Jewish newspaper. At the urging of my friends, I wrote daily, I think in Polish, which was then translated into Yiddish. We ventured into the Italian countryside and observed the poor, the wonderful, the passionate and compassionate Italian villagers in their different endeavours.

We were waiting for a ship and permits to sail to Eretz Yisrael. Touches of levity entered our minds. Our conversations began to turn to topics more typical of our age group. Sometimes we played jokes on one another. Haim's group, as well as the girls' group, was taken to the Bari seaport. Before they departed for Palestine we were sent to join them. In the meantime, a correspondence developed between Hadassah, one of the girls in the group, and me. I guess we were both too shy to contact each other while still in Santa Maria. When my group and I joined them in Bari, we still felt awkward, but the ice was broken.

After some time, a ship became available and on November 5, 1945, close to a thousand of us sailed from Taranto, Italy, for the Land of Israel on the *Princess Kathleen*, the last legal ship to do so under the British government's White Paper. Within a few days we arrived at Haifa and were taken to a facility for new arrivals in Atlit, near Netanya. There I sought the advice of Mr. Skulnick, the education officer from the Jewish Brigade, regarding my desire to further my education in mechanics. He was a bit surprised, having known me as the contributor to our own newspaper in Italy.

Most of my group from Italy, as well as most of the girls' group, were directed to Kibbutz Ma'anit. In the end, Haim and I were sent to a school called Ben Shemen, where we were told we could further our education. Ben Shemen was a well-established school within the framework of Youth Aliyah. It also served as a boarding school for Israeli youths. The children in the school were organized in groups according to party affiliation. The day was divided into classes and work, mostly in agriculture. Although we studied Hebrew, our other classes were often cancelled to give us more time to work in the fields.

Ben Shemen, founded in 1927 by Dr. Siegfried Lehmann, had developed different traditions throughout the years and had an excellent reputation. Dr. Jacobson, the director of the school, instituted a tradition of having the whole student body assemble for lunch in the central dining hall. There would be complete silence, followed by a short piano concert. After this, Dr. Jacobson would give a talk, correlating the particular date to something of consequence that had happened to Jews.

On May 8, 1946, Dr. Jacobson spoke about something someone did years ago in Palestine. My Hebrew was adequate by that time, and I listened attentively. After lunch I ventured to remind him that this particular day was the first anniversary of the end of World War II. I thought he would find it useful and mention it the next day. Instead, he turned to face me and, shaking his finger at me, said, "Itzhak, for us in Eretz Yisrael, the war is still going on. The war has not ended." He turned on the spot and left me there, mumbling to myself that if the war had ended only a few days later than it did, I, and who knows how many tens of thousands of others, would have perished.

I had chosen to go to Palestine in part to search for my family, and I did manage to locate the son and the daughter of my relatives the Poznanskis, who had been killed in Zduńska Wola at the beginning of the war. I was also following the list of survivors on the radio program *Ha'Mador Le'hipus Krovim* as they were being announced. I was hoping against hope, since we had all decided during the war that the son and daughter in Israel would be our contact in case of separation.

I was the only one to appear. It took me a very long time, and the realization still continues to this day, that of my entire family – my parents, my grandparents, my brothers, all my uncles and aunts, their spouses, their children, my cousins – I, young and vulnerable, was the only one, the only one, to continue to live when the war ended.

I expected that we few survivors would receive much attention and good will, that there would be an interest in what had been happening while life was flowing normally in other places. Yet neither my friends nor I were asked to relate the stories of what we had witnessed, although at one time I was asked by a group of people from my town to talk about what had happened. I was able to answer a few of their questions about the fate of some of the people they knew. At the end there was silence. Then people began to talk of their own difficulties in Palestine during that period, such as the temporary shortage of sugar, and made other similar statements. I did not understand the mechanics of that active indifference, and without making a conscious decision about it, I did not talk about the Holocaust for more than fifty years, and I generally stayed away from reading on the subject.

I and the other survivors that I met did not realize we had been traumatized. As far as I know, no one offered psychological counselling to my friends and certainly no one offered it to me. I was not aware that one could get counselling until I came to Ben Shemen. Our school was not only an absorption utility for the Youth Aliyah, but, as I mentioned, it also served as a boarding school for local Israeli youngsters. The Israeli children, at least some of them, received regular counselling, but my friends and I were not offered the same.

I stayed at Ben Shemen for around two years. My wish to continue the study of mechanics created a difficulty, as most of the students worked in agriculture, which was not advancing me in my pursuit. The mechanics section of Ben Shemen was not large enough to accommodate all who applied for it, and the local boys had a better chance of being accepted.

I was determined to study somehow, and asked for a transfer to a place that would make it possible. I was refused and remained in limbo for two months, during which time I worked maintaining the cleanliness of our living quarters.

Later, I was summoned to Dr. Jacobson, who directed me to the agro-mechanical department for a one-week trial period. I still have the tool I produced there in that week. Much later, I learned that Dr. Jacobson had advised the head of that department, David Ud, to tell me that I was not suitable for that profession, so that I could be redirected to farming. David insisted that he allow me to continue and did not comply with Dr. Jacobson's request. At my graduation, in Dr. Jacobson's speech to the assembly, he said that the school sometimes makes a mistake and cited my example.

My group was then sent to Kibbutz Ma'abarot, east of Netanya, to prepare for establishing a new kibbutz or help in the development of an existing one. My goal to learn a profession or trade was elusive. I read at random about mechanics, hydraulics, pneumatics, electricity and machinery of all kinds.

In Kibbutz Ma'abarot, a small percentage of each youth group was required to volunteer for active service in the Palmach, an elite section of the paramilitary forces. My friend Reuben Steinhoff, who had been in Switzerland during the war, volunteered. Reuben's father had been an officer in the Yugoslavian army and was on his way to join his son in Palestine. I also volunteered and was accepted by the newly created technical department of the Palmach. Our task was to repair all kinds of broken machines left by the departing British army, as well as to manufacture armaments. This required lots of improvisation, which was very much to my liking.

After the Israeli declaration of independence in 1948, Egypt, along with four other nations, attacked Israel, and I was sent to the Negev. I later learned that Reuben, because of his knowledge of French, was now a commander of a group of French-speaking Moroccan Jews. He and his platoon, after deeds of great bravery, were cruelly and viciously massacred, just as his father arrived in Israel.

Our first task was to defend the Mekorot facilities, the water distribution centre, since water was a critical issue. During this time, I met a contingent of volunteers from Europe. One of them spoke only Polish and French, and in the course of a few days I tried to familiarize him with our surroundings.

One morning we were awakened by falling bombs and packs of leaflets urging us to gather all the armaments that we had. Eight Egyptian cannons on the road were attacking us, shooting over 1,000 twenty-five pounders into the building of the water installation. In my particular dugout, facing the road, we could see the Egyptian soldiers loading their cannons and we could gauge the time when the next cannon would be shot, which made it possible for two people to run to another larger trench and bring back a sack of grenades. We assumed that the cannons were just softening the target before attacking directly. We did not know at that time that the Egyptians would not fight at night because of a certain visual deficiency. As the signal was being given to me and another young Ben Shemen graduate – called Yoske and a half, because of his height – made our run for the grenades.

We both managed to reach the larger dugout, which served as a first aid unit as well, but suddenly Yoske was not moving. On a given signal I grabbed his grenade as well, and on command I reached our trench. Subsequently, two more people were sent to bring additional grenades, and they returned with the sad news that Yoske had died of a heart attack.

The Egyptians were not there in the morning, having moved on. At the end of the day, seven of our people had died. Among them was my new friend, the volunteer from Poland.

On the premises, there was a machine for digging trenches that belonged to a civilian firm. The regular operator had fouled up some of the cables on the machine before abandoning it. I worked on it to restore it to its former normal function, for which I was awarded. I still have the citation I was given for showing initiative.

The installation company continued to function, although the building itself had been peppered with cannon shots. The two barracks we had occupied went up in flames early in the day. Any mementos I had that my relatives had given me were destroyed in the fire.

In December 1948, the Palmach was dissolved and I was transferred to the Air Force, where my talent at solving mechanical problems was welcomed. As soon as the open hostilities ceased, Dr. Jacobson demanded my release from the Air Force in order to employ me as a teacher. This presented difficulties as the Air Force had just been arranging to transfer me to a small airport near Haifa to train as an ordnance officer. Eventually a man named Mokush made my transfer to Ben Shemen possible, after I told him that I craved a civilian life. Mokush knew me from Kibbutz Ma'abarot. He was then in charge of defense, and I had worked with him late into the night on tasks necessary for the defense of the kibbutz. He was now a high-ranking officer in the Air Force.

During the 1948 war, Ben Shemen had relocated to Kfar Vitkin, near the sea, since the old campus was under siege by the Arab Legion, the army of Transjordan. This new school, now named Ben Shemen B, was a previous British Army camp that had been recently vacated by the military. I was brought in to head the department of agromechanics, which was allied with the ORT organization. Suddenly, I had eighty-seven students – one half in the morning and the other in the afternoon. We had absolutely no tools, no materials and no curriculum, but in many ways this was the tenor of the times. I had only several days to be ready to teach an unruly group of youths. I decided to devise an approach quite different – even defiantly so – from the old methods practised everywhere. The school I had attended gave instruction with drudgery.

I took a small group of students to scavenge the equipment left over by the British, and we then cut the different pieces – hard and soft steel, copper, cast iron, springs flat or coiled, bronze, aluminum and anything else of interest – into manageable sizes.

I spent evenings late into the night writing a basic text on metallurgical processes, and printed it up on an old Gestetner machine. Rather than starting with the old aforesaid drudgery, I wanted the students to experience firsthand the malleability of the various metals. I encouraged them to create any kind of shape and to feel that the old adage "unyielding like steel" is only partly valid. As the boys kept busy comparing the shapes they created, they realized they could not build from their little creations. This was the time to demonstrate to them the various systems for welding – electric, acetylene, brazing – and the care necessary for safety. I was available and encouraged questions.

One day, I was told that the inspector from Tel Aviv was going to visit the school the following week, which was encouraging, since up to that point no one from headquarters had appeared or responded to the paucity of basic tools. When the inspector came in and glanced quickly at the class, he came energetically right to my desk in the centre and berated me for not following some procedure that had not been supplied to us in the first place.

I felt that everything I had done up to then would fall apart through this public humiliation. I seem to remember his name was Mr. Segal. What came to mind at that point was a scene from a movie shown to us when I was a student; it was about a Russian *kolkhoz*, a collective farm, and in the scene, a young man was arguing loudly with a young woman who had just entered a hut that served as a school for students of all ages. The teacher took a paperweight perched on her desk, slammed it loudly against her desk and instructed the students to get up and say "Goodbye tovarish! [comrade]." In the movie, the young man snorted and left the room, slamming the door.

I picked up a hammer that was on my desk for getting attention when needed, and I pounded the desk and told the students to say, "Shalom Mr. Segal!" in the middle of his diatribe. Lo and behold, Mr. Segal snorted and left the room, slamming the door behind him.

From that point on, there was unity rather than blind discipline in my relationship to the students. But this was not a simple matter. After several weeks, the general manager of the school and I were called to the headquarters in Tel Aviv, where a couple of grim-faced people were talking about the absolute unacceptability of raising a voice to an inspector in front of his students. Not having anything to lose, I replied that it is absolutely wrong to yell at a teacher in front of his students. I saw a fleeting smile cross the face of my manager. I was asked to leave the room. Sometime later the manager and I made our way back to the school. Within a few weeks I received the status of permanence, which I did not have before, and a raise in my wages.

As supplies trickled in, I decided to go through the whole year of teaching with my novel sequence. Every student was invited to se-lect one of the agricultural machines in the field and measure the different mechanisms in order to build a model to scale. Despite the heat of the Israeli days it was interesting but hard work, and my stu-dents were usually elated with the task. Eventually they became ex-cited and proud of their productions. Through this activity, I taught the purpose of thorough measurements and the utility of making proper sketches and drawings, and the students benefitted from their co-operation.

I stayed at my job for close to three years and was amused when I heard that a school in France had adopted my approach to teach-ing. I was given a nicely built Swedish wooden hut to live in, perched on a cliff, overlooking the sea. To reach the beach itself it was neces-sary to find a kind of passage carved out by the occasional rain. Of-ten I would see one of the young teachers going down to the beach

and immersing herself in reading a book. In the evening, the younger
teachers would spend the time conversing, telling jokes and danc-
ing. I noticed that the female teachers would talk about the details of
their work and occasionally, when there was a dispute, they always
came to the conclusion to ask one of the girls, named Miriam, for her
opinion. I eventually met Miriam Fluk, who, it turned out, was the
girl who daily went down to the beach to read a book. We became
close friends and enjoyed each other's company. She was called up
to the army, but we continued to communicate by letter or, on occasion, meeting in person. On July 5, 1955, Miriam and I got married
in Tel Aviv.

Instruments of Survival

In 1956, Miriam and I had an opportunity to travel to North America and, wanting to explore the possibility of a new place, we decided to go to Montreal. Within a week of our arrival I started to work in a plant that produced precision gauges necessary for the production of airplane parts and other items. My starting wage was one dollar an hour, which was fine with me. Within a short time I was paid five dollars an hour, and then, once I acquired the ability to speak English, I was given more responsibility and a salary of $20,000 a year.

When our children were born – Mark in 1960 and Vivian in 1963 – our financial needs increased and, feeling that there was no secure future in this company in which I had worked almost ten years, I decided to open my own company. With very limited resources, I rented a basement, purchased a few basic metalworking machines and hired two people; my business partner took care of the non-technical paperwork, which allowed me to develop the machines for different industries.

Some prospective customers, learning by word of mouth of my availability, wanted to purchase machinery that they could not find elsewhere. My facility was too small for large pieces, and anyhow I much preferred high-speed machines for the assembly of small components.

I was asked to build some high-speed machine systems that did not exist anywhere yet. For the first time, I felt really fortunate. During my self-education I had acquired enough grounding in various disciplines to design and build different interesting systems and design them with little effort and much excitement. Being a small outfit, I had to refuse some orders from potential customers. In order to expand I had to carefully choose and train workers who could respond to challenges with enthusiasm.

One day my secretary told me that a man had been trying to reach me. Since, at that time, I was advertising for technical personnel who had the potential and enthusiasm to engage in building automatic equipment, I assumed he was another applicant for the job. When he arrived, it turned out that he actually was a Japanese manufacturer. While in Germany at the Hannover Messe, an industrial technology trade fair, he heard about our undertakings in Montreal and decided to search us out by coming here personally. He was embarking on a major expansion of the production of items and talked about his perception of the global market.

After my decision to expand our facilities, I handled the shortage of experienced personnel. Up to that point, each time I built a machine I was in very close contact with a man who would be building alongside me – by the time the machine was finished, we more or less spoke the same language. I would then create a new group of people to help him with the next job. At times, I was building approximately twenty different machines simultaneously; I decentralized everything into small groups, each with its own space and a set of machines necessary for building the different components. At that point there were only my scribbled sketches of what I wanted. I built machines with simplicity of design and flexibility, along with high speed, for companies in distant countries. Three-quarters of my output were used in Japan while the rest went to the United States, Canada, Mexico, Australia, Europe and Africa. All these orders were achieved by word of mouth.

In 1970, during this time of all-out effort, my wife, Miriam, fell ill. After some time, she was diagnosed with cancer and she had to undergo the appropriate treatment. We all preferred for her to be at home.

In late June 1972, after packing the children's clothing for summer camp and entertaining friends for coffee several days later, she did not feel well. We went to the hospital. After she fell asleep, I was advised to go home and return the next day. A few hours into the night of July 2, the phone rang; I was informed that Miriam had passed away in her sleep.

I drove to the camp to bring our children home, and in a forest near the parking lot, the three of us cried like wounded animals. From that time on I saw myself as a father first and foremost, an instrument of survival for the children. I lamented my complete ignorance and lack of competence in taking care of children. I was in touch with a Boston professor, Dr. Weisman, one of the first people to write a book about dying, but received minimal help from him.

Meanwhile, the business was in a critical stage in the larger and more expensive building of the plant. These were the years during which I developed a manner of running rather than walking, and I was simultaneously completely invested in the children's day-to-day needs.

On one occasion, when asked about who I was, without thinking, and incongruously, I said, "I am a father." What I learned from some books and articles was that there should be no limit to reassuring children, but I exaggerated my care in overindulging them. Nevertheless, to their credit, they grew up to be modest, honest, ethical and moral.

As for my own growth, I discovered the healing properties of water. In the mid- to late-1970s I was on vacation in Greece when I became intrigued by a windsurfer. It was the advent of windsurfing, and when I later windsurfed for the first time, in Guadalupe, I found it challenging and exciting. I soon purchased my first board. I also came to love sailing, particularly a lightweight racer called the Hobie Cat 16, and I even acquired a thirty-two-foot race-rigged sailboat.

Sailing and windsurfing invigorate me; being fully absorbed and focused on the water and its movements is like a meditation. Even now, in my eighties, I continue to windsurf when I can. The water takes me where I want to go. It rescues me.

Epilogue

There is a painting by Francisco Goya called *The Third of May*, which shows Napoleon's soldiers about to execute a group of Spanish civilians. This painting intrigues me, and I once bought a reproduction of it. What struck me at first is the total helplessness on the part of the intended victims, in the face of a row of soldiers equipped with firearms and bayonets. One of the soon-to-be executed men, a heroic figure dressed in white, is raising his hands in horror and despair –to no avail. Future victims are crowded all the way back to the castle, people seemingly well fed and well dressed, awaiting their turn to be killed against the rocky wall. There seems to be a universal truth about human beings. Both executioner and victim seem to follow a predictable, unimaginable behaviour: the victims' resigned passivity and a mechanical detachment of the executioners, at best.

There is a common question, either implied or asked directly of Holocaust survivors: "Why did you go like sheep to slaughter?" I have a ready answer but have remained silent. Looking at the *Third of May* painting, I wonder if many people in the generations since that time wanted to ask this question of Goya's painting of the victims. Actually, people resisted whenever possible. My brothers Chaim and Kalman, who are mentioned in the book *A Voice from the Forest* by Nahum Kohn and Howard Roiter, were in circumstances where they could fight the Germans, and they did! They were partisans, like many others; they died fighting, having inflicted losses on the enemy. In different circumstances, they would have been trapped, with no means to fight, and would have had to succumb, as did so many victims of the Holocaust.

In *A Voice from the Forest*, it is written that an argument ensued among the partisans when one wanted to obtain pencils and notebooks to document everything that was going on. Everyone else in the group was focused on revenge, but my brother Kalman agreed with the young partisan and spoke up, saying, "Especially now, when we are avenging our brothers, sisters and parents, we should be writing it down and preserving it." Nahum Kohn, the surviving partisan who co-wrote the book, stated, "I agreed with Kalman, and I said that writing it down would be part of our revenge-taking. We *had* to do it. And we would do it."

Glossary

Aktion (German; pl. *Aktionen*) The brutal roundup of Jews for forced labour, forcible resettlement into ghettos, mass murder by shooting or deportation to death camps.

Auschwitz (German; in Polish, Oświęcim) A town in southern Poland approximately forty kilometres from Krakow, it is also the name of the largest complex of Nazi concentration camps that were built nearby. The Auschwitz complex contained three main camps: Auschwitz I, a slave labour camp built in May 1940; Auschwitz II-Birkenau, a death camp built in early 1942; and Auschwitz-Monowitz, a slave labour camp built in October 1942. In 1941, Auschwitz I was a testing site for usage of the lethal gas Zyklon B as a method of mass killing, which then went into wide usage. Between 1942 and 1944, transports arrived at Auschwitz-Birkenau from almost every country in Europe – hundreds of thousands from both Poland and Hungary, and thousands from France, the Netherlands, Greece, Slovakia, Bohemia and Moravia, Yugoslavia, Belgium, Italy and Norway. As well, more than 30,000 people were deported there from other concentration camps. It is estimated that 1.1 million people were murdered in Auschwitz; approximately 950,000 were Jewish; 74,000 Polish; 21,000 Roma; 15,000 Soviet prisoners of war; and 10,000–15,000 other nationalities. The Auschwitz complex was liberated by the Soviet army in January 1945.

Ben Shemen (Hebrew; literally, rich in oil) A cooperative farming community (moshav) and youth village located in central Israel. A factory for production of oil and soap was established there in 1905, an orphanage in 1906 and an agricultural training farm in 1908. The village was destroyed during World War I but the community managed to re-establish Ben Shemen as a moshav in 1921. In 1927, Siegfried Lehmann (1892–1958), a German-born doctor and educator who had become involved in the Zionist movement, founded an agricultural school. Ben Shemen joined Youth Aliyah in 1934; both the youth village and moshav continue to exist today. *See also* Youth Aliyah.

Blockälteste (also *Blockältester*; German; literally, block elder) Prisoner appointed by the German authorities as barracks supervisor, charged with maintaining order and accorded certain privileges.

British Mandate Palestine The area of the Middle East under British rule from 1923 to 1948, as established by the League of Nations after World War I. During that time, the United Kingdom severely restricted Jewish immigration. The Mandate area encompassed present-day Israel, Jordan, the West Bank and the Gaza Strip.

cheder (Hebrew; literally, room) An Orthodox Jewish elementary school that teaches the fundamentals of Jewish religious observance and textual study, as well as the Hebrew language.

circumcision Removal of the foreskin of the penis. In Judaism, ritual circumcision is performed on the eighth day of a male infant's life in a religious ceremony known as a *brit milah* (Hebrew) or *bris* (Yiddish) to welcome him into the covenant between God and the People of Israel.

Familienlager Also known as the Czech family camp, a section of the Birkenau "quarantine" camp where recent arrivals were housed temporarily; it was reserved for the more than 10,000 Czech-Jewish prisoners who were deported from the Theresienstadt camp between September and December 1943. For approximately six months, in an effort to counteract rumours that the Nazis were massacring Jews, the Czech Jews were accorded privileges such as receiving parcels and writing letters, but they were eventually subjected to the same fate as other prisoners at Birkenau. Thousands were murdered in the gas chambers on March 8 and 9, 1944; in July, after a selection that found only a few thousand of the prisoners fit for forced labour, the rest of the family camp, more than seven thousand Czech Jews, were sent to the gas chambers. *See also* Theresienstadt.

Fuchs, Dora (1914?–?) The head of the Central Secretariat of the Jewish administration in the Lodz ghetto, Fuchs worked with Mordechai Rumkowski. Dora Fuchs was deported to Auschwitz in 1944 and survived the war. *See also* Rumkowski, Mordechai Chaim.

Gottliebova, Dina (1923–2009; also known as Dina Babbitt) A Czech-born artist deported from Theresienstadt to Auschwitz in 1943. When Gottliebova's paintings in the camp's children's barracks came to the attention of the notorious Josef Mengele, he assigned her to paint portraits of Roma prisoners, which she agreed to on the condition that her mother's life be spared. Both women survived Auschwitz, as well as two other concentration camps. After the war, Gottliebova lived briefly in Paris, where she married before immigrating to the United States with her husband, Art Babbitt. In 1973, she was informed by the Auschwitz-Birkenau State Museum that several of her portraits existed in its collection. She sought to have them returned to her, but the museum refused, insisting on the primacy of the paintings' educational and documentary value. Gottliebova's fight for ownership endured for three decades, and although the case went before a US congressional hearing and had the support of artists, museum curators and Holocaust organization directors, the museum would not relinquish its claim. *See also* Mengele, Josef; Theresienstadt.

Gunskirchen A subcamp of the Mauthausen-Gusen complex that was built in December 1944 and held more than 16,000 Hungarians, hundreds of political prisoners and, in April 1945, thousands of Jews who had been evacuated from the Mauthausen camp. The camp, located in Upper Austria, north of the town of Gunskirchen, outside the village of Edt bei Lambach, operated from December 1944 to May 1945. It was immensely overcrowded and unsanitary; between two hundred and three hundred inmates died each day from typhoid fever and dysentery. Gunskirchen was liberated by American troops on May 4, 1945. *See also* Mauthausen.

Gypsies The term for the Sinti and Roma people commonly used in the past and now generally considered to be derogatory. The Sinti and Roma are a nomadic people who speak Romani, an Indo-European language. During the Holocaust, which the Roma refer to in Romani as the *Porajmos* (the devouring), they were stripped of their citizenship under the Nuremberg Laws and were targeted for death under Hitler's race policies. In Auschwitz-Birkenau, more than 20,000 Sinti and Roma were segregated into the "Gypsy camp" and then systematically murdered. The estimation of how many Roma were killed during World War II varies widely and has been difficult to document – estimations generally range from 200,000 to one million.

hachshara (Hebrew; literally, preparation) A training program to prepare new immigrants for life in the Land of Israel.

Jewish Brigade A battalion that was formed in September 1944 under the command of the British Eighth Army. The Jewish Brigade included more than 5,000 volunteers from Palestine. After the war, the Brigade was essential in helping Jewish refugees and organizing their entry into Palestine. It was disbanded by the British in 1946.

Kanada *Kommando* A prisoner work detail in Auschwitz given the task of sorting through the belongings and clothing confiscated from newly arrived prisoners. The name, adopted by the prisoners working there, came from the widely held belief that Canada was a land of wealth, thus its association with the enormous amount of goods seized by the camp authorities. The warehouses that stored the goods were also referred to as Kanada.

kapo (German) A concentration camp prisoner appointed by the SS to oversee other prisoners as slave labourers.

kibbutz (Hebrew) A collectively owned farm or settlement in Israel, democratically governed by its members. *See also hachshara.*

kolkhoz (Russian) Short for *kollektivnoe khozyaistvo*, a collective farm operated on state-owned land in the USSR. The *kolkhoz* was the dominant form of agricultural enterprise in the former Soviet Union.

Lagerälteste (German; literally, camp elder) A camp inmate in charge of the prisoner population who reported to the SS *Rapportführer* (Report Leader). *See also Rapportführer.*

Lodz Ghetto A restricted area for Jews in the Bałuty district of the Polish city of Lodz. It was the second-largest ghetto in German-occupied Eastern Europe, after the Warsaw ghetto. The ghetto was sealed off on May 1, 1940, with a population of more than 160,000 Jews. Initially intended as a temporary holding place for the Jews of Lodz until they could be deported, its organizational structure served as a model for the establishment of other ghettos. Most of the ghetto inhabitants worked as slave labourers in factories, primarily in the textile industry. The dissolution of the Lodz ghetto began in the summer of 1944 with the deportation of most of its inhabitants to the Chelmno death camp or Auschwitz. The few who remained were liberated by the Soviet Red Army in January 1945. The Lodz ghetto outlasted all the other ghettos established by the Nazis in Eastern Europe. *See also* Rumkowski, Mordechai Chaim.

Mauthausen A notoriously brutal Nazi concentration camp located about twenty kilometres east of the Austrian city of Linz. First established in 1938 shortly after the annexation of Austria to imprison "asocial" political opponents of the Third Reich, the camp grew to encompass fifty nearby subcamps and became the largest forced labour complex in the German-occupied territories. By the end of the war, close to 200,000 prisoners had passed through the Mauthausen forced labour camp system and almost 120,000 of them died there – including 38,120 Jews – from starvation, disease and hard labour. Mauthausen was classified as a Category III camp, which indicated the harshest conditions, and inmates were often worked to death in the brutal Weiner-Graben stone quarry. The US army liberated the camp on May 5, 1945.

Mengele, Josef (1911–1979) The most notorious of about thirty SS garrison physicians in Auschwitz. Mengele was stationed at the camp from May 1943 to January 1945; from May 1943 to August 1944, he was the medical officer of the Birkenau "Gypsy Camp"; from August 1944 until Auschwitz was evacuated in January 1945, he became Chief Medical Officer of the main infirmary camp in Birkenau. One of the camp doctors responsible for deciding which prisoners were fit for slave labour and which were to be immediately sent to the gas chambers, Mengele was also known for conducting sadistic experiments on Jewish and Roma prisoners, especially twins.

Mischling (German; pl. *Mischlinge*; literally, crossbreed) A term used during World War II to denote Germans who were of only partial "Aryan" ancestry and therefore subject to persecution under Hitler's racial policies enacted as the Nuremberg Laws. The edicts included a legal test to determine whether someone was a *Mischling* and, if so, the "degree" or category that defined his or her status.

Palmach (Hebrew acronym for Plugot Machatz; literally, strike forces) A military brigade in British Mandate Palestine that was established in 1941 and initially served as a support for the British Army. In the fall of 1942, the British army ordered the Palmach to be disbanded and it instead went underground, becoming an independent defence force until the modern state of Israel was founded in 1948.

partisans Members of irregular military forces or resistance movements formed to oppose armies of occupation. During World War II there were a number of different partisan groups that opposed both the Nazis and their collaborators in several countries.

The term partisan could include highly organized, almost para-military groups such as the Red Army partisans; ad hoc groups bent more on survival than resistance; and roving groups of bandits who plundered what they could from all sides during the war. There were members of both Polish and Jewish resistance groups who hid out in forests and depended on the cooperation of farmers for food and shelter. There were several Polish resistance movements, often fiercely opposed to one another on ideological grounds, and at least one, the National Armed Forces, was violently antisemitic.

Rapportführer (German; literally, report leader) An SS officer who acted as commander of the overseers of concentration camps barracks. The *Rapportführer* also conducted roll calls and disciplined prisoners, often in a brutal manner.

Rumkowski, Mordechai Chaim (1877–1944) The chief administrator of the Lodz ghetto, appointed by the German authorities as head of the Jewish Council (or "Elder of the Jews"). Rumkowski was in charge of all the Jewish public agencies and institutions in the ghetto, as well as the Jewish police. He also replaced German currency with special ghetto money, signed by himself, that came to be known as "Rumkies." Rumkowski was – and remains – a somewhat controversial figure because of his decisions to cooperate with the Germans in order to serve what he felt were the best interests of the Lodz ghetto inhabitants. Rumkowski served in this capacity from the time that the ghetto was established on February 8, 1940, until its dissolution in the summer of 1944, when he was deported to Auschwitz.

Schreibstube (German) An administrative office.

Sonderkommando (German; special unit) Concentration camp prisoners ordered to remove corpses from the gas chambers, load them into the crematoria and dispose of the remains. On October 7, 1944, *Sonderkommando* workers coordinated an attempt to destroy the crematoria facilities at Auschwitz-Birkenau.

Sosnowiec (also known as Sosnowitz II) A subcamp of Auschwitz opened in May 1944 to supply workers for the Ost-Maschinenbau GmbH company, manufacturing barrels and shells for anti-aircraft weapons. Most of the prisoners were sent there from Auschwitz and worked in eight- or twelve-hour shifts, assisting civilian workers who operated the machinery. By the end of 1944, there were nine hundred prisoners, 90 per cent of whom were Jewish. The camp was evacuated in January 1945 and its prisoners were sent on a death march to Gleiwitz, then to Troppau (also known as Opawa, then in Bohemia and now in Poland), and then, by train, to the Mauthausen concentration camp. *See also* Mauthausen.

SS (abbreviation of Schutzstaffel; Defence Corps) The SS was established in 1925 as Adolf Hitler's elite corps of personal bodyguards. Under the direction of Heinrich Himmler, its membership grew from 280 in 1929 to 50,000 when the Nazis came to power in 1933, and to nearly a quarter of a million on the eve of World War II. The SS was comprised of the Allgemeine-SS (General SS) and the Waffen-SS (Armed, or Combat SS). The General SS dealt with policing and the enforcement of Nazi racial policies in Germany and the Nazi-occupied countries. An important unit within the SS was the Reichssicherheitshauptamt (RSHA, the Central Office of Reich Security), whose responsibility included the Gestapo (Geheime Staatspolizei). The SS ran the concentration and death camps, with all their associated economic enterprises, and also fielded its own Waffen-SS military divisions, including some recruited from the occupied countries.

Theresienstadt (German) A walled town in the Czech Republic sixty kilometres north of Prague that served as both a ghetto and a concentration camp. More than 73,000 Jews from the German Protectorate of Bohemia and Moravia and from the Greater German Reich (including Austria and parts of Poland) were deported to Theresienstadt between 1941 and 1945, 60,000 of whom were deported to Auschwitz or other death camps. Theresienstadt was showcased as a "model" ghetto for propaganda purposes to demonstrate to delegates from the International Red Cross and others the "humane" treatment of Jews and to counter information reaching the Allies about Nazi atrocities and mass murder. Theresienstadt was liberated on May 8, 1945 by the Soviet Red Army.

Youth Aliyah A child rescue organization founded in Berlin in 1933 by Recha Freier (1892–1984), a teacher, poet and musician. Shortly after the Nazi rise to power, Freier worked to bring Jewish children and teenagers to safety in British Mandate Palestine and Great Britain. Youth Aliyah continues to operate villages for children in Israel today.

Zionism A movement promoted by the Viennese Jewish journalist Theodor Herzl, who argued in his 1896 book *Der Judenstaat* (The Jewish State) that the best way to resolve the problem of antisemitism and persecution of Jews in Europe was to create an independent Jewish state in the historic Jewish homeland of Biblical Israel. Zionists also promoted the revival of Hebrew as a Jewish national language. In interwar Poland, Zionism was one of many Jewish political parties with affiliated schools and youth groups.

Zionist Organizations Among the significant Jewish political movements that flourished in Poland before World War II were various Zionist parties – the General Zionists; the Labour Zionists (Poale Zion); the Revisionist Zionists formed under Ze'ev Jabotinsky; and the Orthodox Religious Zionists (the Mizrachi movement) – and the entirely secular and socialist Jewish Workers' Alliance, known as the Bund. Although Zionism and Bundism were both Jewish national movements and served as Jewish political parties in interwar Poland, Zionism advocated a Jewish national homeland in the Land of Israel, while Bundism advocated Jewish cultural autonomy in the Diaspora. A significant number of Polish Jews in the interwar years preferred to affiliate with the non-Zionist religious Orthodox party, Agudath Israel. *See also* Zionism.

Photographs

The only pre-war photo Eddie has of his family. From left to right: Eddie's father, Samuel; Eddie; Eddie's brother Kalman; his brother Chaim; and his mother, Hela. Sieradz, date unknown.

1 A page from the official Residents' Registration Book in the Lodz ghetto, showing the list of people residing at the Rumkowski residence on Hanseatenstrasse 63. Icchok (Eddie) Klein is listed second from the bottom. Circa 1942. Courtesy of the Center for Jewish Research at the University of Lodz.

2 Eddie Klein's death certificate, erroneously issued in Mauthausen, 1945.

1

2

1 A photo in an Israeli newspaper showing Eddie inspecting a student's work at Ben Shemen school B. Kfar Vitkin, Netanya, 1949.

2 Eddie supervising his students, 1949.

1

2

1 Eddie (back row, fourth from the left) with students at Ben Shemen. Circa 1950.
2 With Ben Shemen students in the early 1950s. Eddie is standing fourth from the right.

Miriam Fluk, Eddie's future wife, 1950.

Eddie and Miriam's wedding photo. Tel Aviv, July 5, 1955.

Eddie and Miriam with their children, Mark and Vivian, on the construction site of Eddie's future factory, circa 1968.

1 & 2 Eddie and his son, Mark, at the Western Wall on the occasion of Mark's bar
mitzvah. Jerusalem, 1973.

3 Eddie, Mark and Vivian in the Old City. Jerusalem, 1973.

1

2

3

1 Eddie (right) in the factory he built for miniature automation. Montreal, circa
   1970.
2 & 3 Two of the many high-speed automation machines that Eddie built during his
   career.

Eddie on a Hobie Cat 16 in the 1980s.

3

1 Eddie and family in Montreal, 2013. In the back row, left to right: Eddie's grand-sons, Doron, Gilad and Adam; in front, left to right: Eddie's daughter, Vivian; his daughter-in-law, Jan; his son, Mark; and Eddie.

2 Family in Montreal, 2014. Left to right: Eddie's son-in-law, Itzhak, Doron, Eddie, Adam, Vivian and Gilad.

3 Eddie with his granddaughter, Hannah, and his daughter-in-law, Jan. Montreal, 2013.

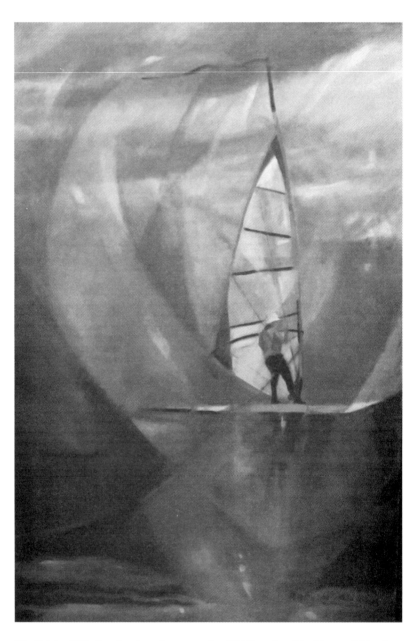

The Spirit of Windsurfing (2005), a portrait of Eddie painted by his good friend Rita Briansky.

Index

The Azrieli Foundation was established in 1989 to realize and extend the philanthropic vision of David J. Azrieli, C.M., C.Q., M.Arch. The Foundation's mission is to support a wide spectrum of initiatives in education and research. The Azrieli Foundation is an active supporter of programs in the fields of Education, the education of architects, scientific and medical research, and the arts. The Azrieli Foundation's many initiatives include: the Holocaust Survivor Memoirs Program, which collects, preserves, publishes and distributes the written memoirs of survivors in Canada; the Azrieli Institute for Educational Empowerment, an innovative program successfully working to keep at-risk youth in school; the Azrieli Fellows Program, which promotes academic excellence and leadership on the graduate level at Israeli universities; the Azrieli Music Project, which celebrates and fosters the creation of high-quality new Jewish orchestral music; and the Azrieli Neurodevelopmental Research Program, which supports advanced research on neurodevelopmental disorders, particularly Fragile X and Autism Spectrum Disorders.